Soaring in the Spirit

Soaring in the Spirit

Rediscovering Mystery
in the Christian Life

Charles J. Conniry, Jr.

LONDON • COLORADO SPRINGS • HYDERABAD

First published 2007 by Authentic Media
9 Holdom Avenue, Bletchley, Milton Keynes, Bucks,
MK1 1QR, UK
1820 Jet Stream Drive, Colorado Springs, CO 80921, USA
OM Authentic Media, Medchal Road, Jeedimetla Village,
Secunderabad 500 055, A.P., India
www.authenticmedia.co.uk

Authentic Media is a division of IBS-STL UK, a company limited by
guarantee (registered charity no. 270162)

British Library Cataloguing in Publication Data

A catalogue record for this book is available from the
British Library

ISBN 13: 978-1-84227-508-5
ISBN-10: 1-85078-508-9

Design by James Kessell for Scratch the Sky Ltd
(www.scratchthesky.com)
Print Management by Adare Carwin
Printed and bound in Great Britain by J.H. Haynes & Co., Sparkford

To my soaring partner, Dianne Conniry

Contents

Faith in an Emerging Culture
Series Preface

Series Editor Pete Ward

It is common knowledge that Western culture has undergone major changes and we now find ourselves in an increasingly postmodern (or post-postmodern?), post Christendom, post industrial, post-just-about-anything-you-like world. The church now sits on the margins of western culture with a faith 'package deal' to offer the world that is perceived as out of date and irrelevant. How can we recontextualize the old, old story of the gospel in the new, new world of postmodernity? How can we fulfill our missional calling in a world that cannot any longer understand or relate to what we are saying? 'Faith in an Emerging Culture' seeks to imaginatively rethink Christian theology and practice in postmodern ways. It does not shrink from being explorative, provocative and controversial but is at the same time committed to remaining within the bounds of orthodox Christian faith and practice. Most readers will find things to agree with and things which will irritate them but we hope at very least to provoke fresh thought and theological/spiritual renewal.

Foreword

Chuck Conniry is a brilliant thinker and a gifted writer. To explain this observation, I refer the reader to Jean Leclercq's theory of "mutation," which interprets the historical process as moving either by evolution or mutation. On a personal level, such a mutation requires a unique creativity that gives inventive power both to the past and the future. The author is a mutational man, one whose awareness has transformed into a new form of consciousness.

In his professional training and career, from his legalistic background in the Roman Catholic Church, through a marathon of pastoral ministry in evangelical churches, to his PhD from Fuller Seminary in California, Conniry has developed into a multidimensional man, a philosopher and a man of prayer, a theologian sensitive to mystical intuition and highly skilled in rational speculation. In this remarkable man the great spiritual traditions converge, making him heir to the spiritual heritage of humankind.

In reading his manuscript, I am reminded of a passage in the Gospel of Mark: "Jesus went home again and such a crowd collected that they could not even have a meal. When his relatives heard of this, they set out to take charge of him, convinced he was out of his mind" (3:20, 21).

Critics may protest that Conniry has watered down the gospel in the chapter on Messy Spirituality (which is worth the price of the book), and that his cheese has slid off his cracker. Truth be told, the writer offers enormous consolation to those who have been misled by the myth, "once converted, fully verted." Its premise is that once you are saved, you will never experience envy or jealousy, never lose your temper and never be troubled by inordinate sexual desires. This false teaching has caused incalculable harm to sincere believers and created the impression that once you accept Jesus as Lord, you become the equivalent of a patient anesthetized on the operating table.

As personal experience has taught me, I continue to stumble and fall in the undulating rhythm of my imperfect life. In the seventh chapter of his letter to the Romans, the Apostle Paul told us not to be surprised. Grace and failure coexist in the same life.

Conniry explores Dallas Willard's concept of "sin management" and its tragic consequence – rampant dishonesty in so many of our churches. Years ago, I started a group called *The Notorious Sinners*. Our first meeting was in New Orleans. One guy from Portland, Oregon lamented, "Why do I have to come half way across the country to share personal stuff that I can't say in my own church for fear of being kicked out?"

The author's treatment of modernism, postmodernism and "most-modernism" is a philosophical and theological gem. For me, one of the great delights of the book is Conniry's stories. I laughed, cried, and had an occasional attack of the happies.

This book can be read with profit by believers and unbelievers, philosophers and theologians, pastors and lay people, and anyone who longs to soar in the Spirit.

Brennan Manning

Preface

This book is about experiencing the presence of Jesus Christ in the moment-by-moment "nows" of daily life. I do not romanticize the spiritual life by promising that our journey of faith is marked by unbroken, upward progress or that intimacy with Christ leads to a more fulfilling end. Life in the Spirit does not always take us where we want to go. I do not idealize life in Christ by suggesting that the way of the cross holds the key to "spiritual success," nor do I minimize the complexities and paradoxes of the Christian life by distilling them into a simple formula that is readily understood and easily applied.

Most people pick up a book on the spiritual life because they believe the subject to be important for more than academic reasons. This is not a work aimed at convincing you that you need what you do not want. Its aim is to provide a vocabulary to describe the deep yearnings that you already sense intuitively.

There are several significant assumptions that underlie this work, all of which speak to the issue of voice. I am speaking to those who consider themselves followers of Jesus Christ. Accordingly, this piece is not an argument for the truthfulness of the Christian faith. I am targeting those who want to learn something they might not already know. Therefore I delve deeply into the subject matter at certain points, but hopefully not so deeply that I lose or frustrate those who enjoy the lighter parts of the story. I am speaking to those who are informed but not necessarily theologically educated. So I do my best to avoid ivory-tower prose.

Others of course are welcome to listen in and glean what they can. But this book is aimed at specific conversation partners: those who have made a profession of faith, in most cases many years ago, and have experienced their fair share of personal letdowns in the intervening seasons of life, some of the most profound of which have been perpetrated by fellow churchgoers. Moreover, I have of necessity written this piece from my own place in the world – a North American setting – though it is my prayer that disciples in other places will find points of convergence with their own contexts.

My doctoral mentor, James Wm. McClendon, Jr., taught me that the first task of theology is to locate our place in the story. We cannot get to our desired destination unless we first get our bearings and pinpoint our current location on the map. Think of the directions stationed at various points in a shopping mall. In every instance the phrase, "you are here," highlighted by a brightly colored arrow, is an indispensable aid in helping us find our way. Everybody's life story is different. This book is written from the perspective of my story. It is the only vantage point I have. The book is my attempt at first-person theology, which in truth is the only way any of us do theology – even when we pretend to be doing otherwise. I have tried to locate myself in God's larger story without looking like more of a narcissist than I actually am. And I have done so in the hope that others would see how together our collective stories intermingle and point us to the "we-are-here" place in God's all-encompassing story of creation, redemption, and glory.

We will explore the reasons why I emphasize "mystery" and "spiritual soaring" as we go. For now it is enough to say, "Welcome to the journey!"

Charles J. Conniry, Jr.
Portland, Oregon
New Year's Day, 2007

Acknowledgments

Long ago the writer of Ecclesiastes made it a matter of public record that there's no such thing in the human realm as pure originality. Each of us is the product of countless influences and influencers. In the final analysis, however, we have to take responsibility for the way we play the hand that life has dealt us. So I must say at the outset that – despite the fingerprints of so many others on this book – what I have written is nobody else's fault but mine. It reflects the good, the bad, and the ugly of all that has contributed to my formation as a follower of Jesus Christ. I don't blame the bad and the ugly for the brokenness I still carry. It belongs to me and no one else.

I do, however, credit the many good people in my life whose love, companionship, forgiveness, and encouragement have made me a better person than I would have been otherwise. At the top of this list are my parents, Chuck, Sr. and Shirley Conniry; the wife of my youth, Dianne; and my three great children, Krystal, Matthew, and Nathan. I am also blessed to count my beloved colleagues at George Fox Evangelical Seminary among those who are nearest and dearest to me – Larry Shelton, Kent Yinger, MaryKate Morse, Jules Glanzer, Steve Delamarter, Dan Brunner, Carole Spencer, Laura Simmons, Mark Weinert, Sheila Bartlett, Gloria Doherty, Charlie Kamilos, Jean Borgman, and the two people without whom I would not survive as director of the seminary's Doctor of Ministry program: Loren Kerns and Dee Small.

My wife, Dianne, more than any other person, helped me find my voice as a writer. Higher education left me with a set of writing skills that was both sharp and sterile. I learned to communicate in the dispassionate language of the academy – a language that is devoid of color and personality. When I would let Dianne sample things I had written in that dialect, she would say, "Why can't you just write the way you speak? Nobody wants to wade through material like that. It's not you. Who are you trying to talk to?"

The truth is I wanted to talk to her – and to everybody else like her. After several years of trying, I finally started to produce material that she liked to read. My hunch was that if she liked it, maybe others would too. So after I finished the first four chapters of this book, I sent them to Dr. Robin Parry, editorial director of Paternoster Press, who (foolishly or not) had already agreed to publish the finished product. His feedback was prompt and to the point. In a word, he liked what I had written and told me to continue as I had begun. His encouragement was nothing less than Jesus' confirmation that I was on the right path.

My friend, Dr. Frank Green, was the third person to read the manuscript in its pre-published form. Frank is not only well read. More than twenty years my friend, he is also faithful enough to tell me what he really thinks of my work. He helped me believe that I had something worthwhile to say. For that I am most grateful.

I am particularly grateful to my friend, Brennan Manning, who encouraged me to "finish the book, come what may." His foreword made me cry the first time I read it. My longtime friend, Dave Swelland, was also a source of constant encouragement. I thank my friends, Len Sweet, Ray Anderson, Sally Morgenthaler, and MaryKate Morse for being gracious enough to interrupt their busy schedules long enough to read the draft manuscript and write some very nice things for the back cover. I am thankful to others who read portions of this manuscript and offered indispensably valuable feedback, including my colleagues, Carole Spencer and Laura Simmons, Darla Samuelson, my former administrative assistant, my friends Roger Button, George Hemmingway, and Sam Rima, and the many students at George Fox Evangelical Seminary whose feedback was both gracious and constructive.

I also want to thank Dr. Lawrence Osborn for his careful editing of the manuscript and the administration of George

Fox University for granting me a sabbatical in which to put the finishing touches on this piece.

Charles J. Conniry, Jr.

1. Life After God

O God, you are my God, earnestly I seek you; my soul thirsts for you, my body longs for you, in a dry and weary land where there is no water.

My soul will be satisfied as with the richest of foods; With singing lips my mouth will praise you.

My soul clings to you; your right hand upholds me.

Psalm 63:1, 5, 8

When we are called to follow Christ, we are summoned to an exclusive attachment to his person. The grace of his call bursts all the bonds of legalism. It is a gracious call, a gracious commandment.

Dietrich Bonhoeffer, *The Cost of Discipleship*

The Smiling Cross

There is a longing that cannot be satisfied by any earthly delight. It is the "hunger and thirst for righteousness" (Matthew 5:6) – a deep yearning for spiritual sustenance, the food and drink of the spirit – that chastens every human heart, though not all recognize it as such. While many choose the wide path of earthly indulgence to quench this spiritual ache, others see the light and confront it head on, on its own terms, for what it truly is: *the human being's inborn drive to be in a life-embracing relationship with its Creator.* So begins the journey. We embrace the truth that Jesus Christ is the Savior of humanity and enter New Life – brimming with promise and hope and eager expectation. At least that's the simple version. Seldom, however, is the faith journey so neat and clean.

Like many, my faith journey began in stages. My earliest memory of God came out of a meaningful conversation with my mother. I was three or four years old. She was trying to teach me the Lord's Prayer: "Our Father who art in heaven, hallowed be thy name . . ." I stopped her in mid sentence, "Who is God?" As an elementary school teacher my mother was adept at recognizing key teaching opportunities. She removed a crucifix from the hallway wall where we were standing and knelt down beside me, at eye level.

She pointed to the figure nailed to the cross and said softly, unforgettably, "This is God." The tiny body and the cross to which it was affixed appeared, in the eyes of a child, as a single cruciform image. God was a cross. She told me that God is all knowing and all powerful. He is without beginning and without end – and he is everywhere at all times. He knows my thoughts, so I do not even have to say my prayers out loud. He is pleased when I do what is right and saddened when I do what is wrong.

It was more than I could take in all at once. I went to my room and lay on the bed (it was naptime). I pictured God for the first time – a cross floating in the air. In my newfound knowledge that there was no need to speak audibly, I thought to God silently, "I love you." The crossbeam turned upward. God was . . . *smiling*. He was pleased. I recall several other instances in the weeks that followed in which my behavior was less praiseworthy. At such times I saw the crossbeam droop downward. God was disappointed. The image of a cruciform God faded over time, but growing up in a Roman Catholic home – and attending private Catholic schools from first grade through high school – made it impossible to escape the fact of God's presence.

One morning when I was in second grade, the Sisters of St. Joseph worked to prepare us for our First Communion, which entailed, of necessity, First Confession. We began the day with a tour of the confessional booth – a dark, musty place whose hard kneelers creaked with the slightest movement, broadcasting every tremor of fear to the daunting presence on the other side of the screen. We were ushered one by one into the windowless, closet-like chamber with instructions to kneel for several, long minutes . . . alone in the dark silence. The goal of this dry run was, ostensibly, to help us feel more at ease with the real thing. Afterwards we returned to the classroom for a briefing on "sin."

I discovered that there were two kinds of sin — "mortal sin" and "venial sin." According to the *Catechism of the Catholic Church*, a person is guilty of mortal sin when he or she deliberately chooses, "both knowing it and willing it – something gravely contrary to the divine law and to the ultimate end of man . . ."[1] If one dies in a state of unabsolved mortal sin, he or she faces the sure sentence of eternal damnation. Less serious infractions are called "venial sins." Although "deliberate and unrepented venial sin disposes us little by little to commit mortal sin . . . [it] does not set us in direct opposition to the will and friendship of God; it does not break the covenant with God. With God's grace it is humanly reparable." Unlike its mortal counterpart, "venial sin does not deprive the sinner of sanctifying grace, friendship with God, charity, and consequently eternal happiness."[2] But knowing so much about sin only deepened the confusion. How could I know if I was guilty of mortal sin or venial sin?

In addition to the scintillating lesson on sin that morning, the class was briefed on the mechanics of receiving First Communion. We were told when and where to line up. We rehearsed our response to the priest's eucharistic pronouncement, "The body of Christ." We were to reply, "Amen," which is to say that we agreed with the declaration that the wafer we were receiving onto our tongues was in truth the transubstantiated flesh of Christ. (We didn't get to partake of Christ's blood, which retained a 12 percent alcohol content from its pre-transubstantiated state.) Then came recess.

Still pondering the morning's classroom experiences, I ventured out to the playground with a bag of potato chips. No sooner had I opened the bag than a classmate ran up to mooch a chip. What occurred next would become a significant event, permanently etched in memory. Without forethought, I removed a chip from the bag and held it before him in eucharistic pose. "The body of Christ," I pronounced. Delighted, he replied, "Amen!" Several other children witnessed this and immediately fell into line. Before I knew it, half the playground had lined up to confess that Jesus was a potato chip. Unfortunately the children at recess were not the only ones to witness this profane celebration. After recess a new word was introduced to our vocabulary – *sacrilege*.

The playground attendants considered this so serious a transgression that they summoned Monsignor Van Vegel, the parish's chief rector. The Monsignor stood vigil at the front of the classroom as we filed in from the playground, sternly eying each soul that passed through the door. Monsignor Van Vegel had struck me as a kind and gentle man in past encounters. But in that moment his gray hair was white hot. His black, ankle-length clerical robe, festooned with bright red buttons from collar to hem, radiated ecclesiastical authority. He spoke with an Irish brogue that made his words all the more memorable: "I heard that something very, very bad happened at recess today. Several of you – *and one boy in particular* [waving his index finger and looking at me] – committed sacrilege." I didn't know if the feeling that overtook me was my heart coming up into my throat or sinking into my bowels. Monsignor Van Vegel went on to explain what sacrilege was and to warn us never to let this happen again. But he assured us that as bad as it was to mock what was holy, it was not done deliberately. *It was a venial sin*. He suggested that we include this offense with the other sins we would be rehearsing at First Confession. Then he left . . . without imposing any additional consequences.

The potato chip incident was a memorable event for reasons other than Monsignor Van Vegel. To my recollection, it is the only time I could say for certain that I had committed a *venial sin*. So far as I could tell, I committed every other sin *knowingly* and *willfully*. To make matters worse, I learned from subsequent visits to the confessional booth that many of the sins I committed regularly were considered "serious offenses" – and since I now knew that, I could not claim venial culpability. I concluded that I had to be guilty of nothing less than mortal sin.

Weekly confession eventually forced me into a deadly dilemma. Rather than endure the shame and humiliation of confessing mortal sin on a weekly basis – no less to the same priest who surely could not forget me (no one else's sins could possibly have been so loathsome) – I hid my guilt behind a sterile rehearsing of the Ten Commandments: "Father, forgive me, for I have sinned. It has been one week since my last confession and these are my sins. I broke the Second Commandment five times . . ." (which in the Catholic version of the Commandments is, "You shall not take the name of the Lord your God in vain"). I found it easier to admit that I broke a number than to confess that I had repeatedly (many more times than five, in fact) said, "God damn it!" It was far less humiliating to say, "I broke Number Seven" ("You shall not steal") than to admit that I had stolen five dollars from my father's wallet that week. And it was preferable by far to say that I violated the sixth Commandment ("You shall not commit adultery") than to confess the shameful truth that I had masturbated. The priest closed the session with the imposition of penance – to be carried out immediately afterward (it typically consisted of praying three or four "Our Fathers" and "Hail Marys") – and the pronouncement of absolution. Each week was the same. I left confession with the soul-wrenching conviction that while I had lied to a priest I could not hide from God. And since I had not in fact confessed, I was not in truth forgiven. I stood guilty of mortal sin.

I eventually stopped going to confession. There seemed little point to it. Church attendance gradually ended as well. At age thirteen I added a new wrinkle to the Sunday morning routine. I walked to church each week, as I had done for several years, but instead of entering the sanctuary I spent the hour sitting outside on the steps. That way I could satisfactorily answer my mother's faithful query: "Did you go to church like I asked?" "Yes, Mom," I dutifully replied, "I went to church." I completed the rest of the sentence under by breath, " . . . but I didn't go *into* church." Not long after that I started sneaking booze from my father's liquor cabinet. I smoked my first joint at fourteen. By the time I turned eighteen I could not start or finish a day without smoking marijuana. Since alcohol and marijuana had become daily staples, I would spice things up every so often with more exotic drugs like "uppers," "downers," cocaine, or hallucinogens like LSD or "magic" (psilocybin) mushrooms. My mother knew I was spiritually adrift. Still every Sunday she would pose the faithful question, "Did you go to church today, Chuck?" "Yes, Mom," lying, "I went to church." Gone were the days of the smiling cross.

Visitor of the Soul

The curtain was opened on another stage of my faith journey in summer of my twentieth year. It was a beautiful sunny morning in La Jolla, California – approximately 11 a.m. I had just rolled out of bed. Nine months earlier I had walked away from a good job to pursue my dream of playing keyboards in a rock band. I spent my nights getting high and playing music. My spending money came from unemployment checks that I collected because I was able to convince the agency that my employer had fired me. I stretched that income further by selling marijuana, which gave me a free supply of the narcotic – so long as I smoked just enough of the surplus to break even. That plan worked until I was pulled over one night for a burned-out headlight. The police officer smelled alcohol on my breath and searched the car. He found several one-ounce bags of marijuana and several hundred dollars of cash in my pocket. I was arrested for "possession of marijuana with the intent to sell." I dodged prison by opting to participate in a three-month open-door recovery program. I had finished the program a month before and life had started to settle back into a normal routine. I would play and party late into the night and make my way home around 3:00 or 4:00 in the morning.

By the time I got up that day my parents had long departed for work. The house was quiet. I fixed a cup of coffee and returned upstairs to roll a joint from the fresh stash of homegrown that I had acquired earlier in the week.

My bedroom's exterior door opened onto a large upper deck with a panoramic view of the surrounding neighborhood below. I had grown up in privileged circumstances. I knew that. The sun was warm on my face and arms. The day was ⁣⁣⁣⁣⁣⁣ ⁣⁣⁣⁣ ⁣⁣⁣⁣⁣⁣ ⁣⁣⁣⁣ ⁣⁣⁣⁣⁣⁣ clear blue. White and pink oleander blossoms mingled with lush, variegated greenery. Lawnmowers buzzed in the distance. Late-morning birds busily chirped in the trees to my left and right, as if engaged in intense conversation. The light breeze was caressing and fresh. It was paradise. I lit the freshly rolled joint and drew the first hit deep into my lungs – holding it there for several long seconds and then opening my throat to let the smoke make its rapid escape. I sipped the coffee and said out loud, "I've got it made . . . a gorgeous day, a nice cup of coffee, great weed . . . life doesn't get any better than this." What happened next was life altering.

"Who are you trying to kid?" Like an intruder kicking down the front door, this question burst into my consciousness with such force and clarity that I could pay attention to nothing else. I sat in stunned silence. "Where did that come from?" I wondered. In that moment all other physical and mental activity was suspended. I was captivated by this uninvited-yet-not-unfamiliar caller who had broken into my happy thoughts to deliver the truth that I had willfully ignored. He continued, "You don't have it made at all. Your life is on a dead-end road. If you keep going in the direction you're headed you will end up like Laura and Gary."

Laura was a beautiful young woman who got pregnant when she was sixteen years old. She kept the baby and eventually married the father, an eighteen-year-old drug dealer named Tom. Laura did her best to make a home for her husband and young son, but the drugs were ubiquitous and she liked to party. One night after getting high on "reds" (a barbiturate) Laura aspirated in her sleep and drowned in her own vomit. Gary was my best friend's brother. Everybody that knew Gary loved Gary. He was out with friends one Friday night, getting stoned on "ludes" (methaqualone, a sedative used to tranquilize horses), when the car he was driving veered off the road and plunged down an embankment. Gary had apparently passed out at the wheel. When the paramedics reached his car at the bottom of the ravine, they found him dead. Though he had not sustained life-threatening injuries from the crash, he – like Laura – had suffocated on his own vomit. I was deeply affected by the untimely deaths of these two special human beings. The Visitor of my soul had seized upon the most compelling of examples to signal the gravity of my condition.

I began to reflect on why my life had turned out the way it had. Why, I mused, did I find it impossible to extricate myself from marijuana's grip? Every effort to quit over the past two years had been met with self-deprecating failure. Then it dawned on me. Marijuana was filling a void in my life, and whenever I tried to quit, I had nothing better to put in its place. But what, I wondered, is better than Marijuana? The Visitor gently answered, "I am." The words cascaded over me . . . and into me. I knew he was right. Only God can fill the void.

This exchange brought to mind something Father Aquinas had said to his high-school religion class two years earlier. Father Aquinas was a brilliant – if not patently bizarre – man in his late fifties. He was medium-built in stature, but his booming voice, forceful stare, and commanding stride made him a towering figure. Every evening after school he would pace, ritualistically, back and forth in the school's courtyard with his steely gaze fixed on a small black book (a Bible or prayer book), which he held with arms upstretched, at eye level. It was a strange sight to behold. Whenever I came to class without my textbook, he would bellow the same refrain, "Ha! I see you've come to class again *intellectually naked*." (That was in fact the most peculiar remark I ever heard from a teacher.) The course bore the deceivingly simple title, "Demonology." Even though I received a failing grade for the class, I was riveted by Father Aquinas' lectures. I came away from the class with one point permanently branded on my memory: Satan is more powerful than I am, and the only way to overcome the forces of evil is through the one power in the universe that is greater – *God*.

Clasping coffee cup in one hand and joint in the other, I knew I had come to a crossroads. I could stay on the present course and face certain spiritual bankruptcy or I could heed the Visitor's invitation and begin a whole new life. In that moment of existential crisis there could be only one acceptable alternative. I resolved to fill the hole in my soul with God rather than marijuana.

False Prophet and Faithful Piano Teacher

The decision to enter into a relationship with God included a corresponding resolution: I would seek to become a spiritual person without returning to (what I deemed at that time) the suffocating traditionalism of my Roman Catholic past. I phoned my best friend, Manuel, and informed him that I had decided to make some changes in my life. I knew he would join me in this new endeavor. For months he had been talking about how sick he was of being held hostage to marijuana. Manuel had recently introduced me to a call-in radio program hosted by a self-proclaimed sage named Roy Masters, who headed up the spiritual-but-not-religious organization, "Foundation for Human Understanding."

Mr. Masters taught that the cause of all evil and suffering is the devil, who happens to indwell every person that has not experienced enlightenment. When one invokes the power of God through enlightenment, the devil is forever driven from one's body. Without enlightenment, Mr. Masters warned, one can toil for years to become a good person – all to no avail. The key, he said, was a unique form of meditation that only he could teach. And for a small fee, one could purchase his cassette tapes, which held the secret techniques of this soul-saving practice. Manuel was delighted with my decision and promised to join me in the quest to be liberated from Satan's grip. Within a few days a brown package containing the precious tapes arrived in the mail. My self-improvement program was underway.

The next few weeks witnessed a dramatic change for the good. I was practicing Mr. Masters' meditation techniques and feeling much better about myself. I was a bit troubled by his claim to be the present-day equivalent of Jesus Christ, but not enough to be dissuaded. I had finally gotten my life back. For the first time in years I was free of marijuana's stranglehold. I was managing my anger as never before and felt energized to pursue some new personal goals – one of which was to master my skills as a keyboard player. After all, I reasoned, if I was going to be a rock star, I should have sufficient mastery of my craft. I looked up Mrs. Merriam Baird, a gifted piano teacher from whom I had taken lessons as a boy, and was pleased to discover that she was still giving piano lessons.

When I arrived at Merriam's home for my first lesson I found a different person than I expected. We hadn't seen each other for twelve years. Aside from the predictable signs of aging, Merriam was aglow with a joy that seemed to exude from every pore. The living room walls were adorned with several pieces of art that conveyed distinctively Christian overtones. I surmised that she had become more spiritual since we last met. The conversations that ensued over the next few weeks confirmed my suspicion. She talked openly about her born-again experience and that of her grown children.

One evening I excitedly told her of my self-improvement program and of Roy Masters, the great guru that had taught me so much about spiritual truth. Her face fell and her eyes filled with concern. "Oh, Chuck," she said in a quivering voice, "Roy Masters is a false prophet. He doesn't believe any of the things that Jesus taught." She straightened her back as if to aim the next words straight into my heart, "Honey, you need Jesus." She went on to explain how much Jesus loved me and what great plans he had for my life.

I had never heard God's love described so tenderly and poignantly. As she continued to speak I was overcome with the realization that God had orchestrated everything in my life to bring me to that one conversation. "Wait here," she said, jumping from her seat. She darted from the studio and returned moments later with a small, dark blue book – a New Testament. I strained to hold back the tears. She signed the front page: "To Chuck (with love) from Merriam," and scrolled the date, September 29, 1977. She counseled me to start with the Gospel of John and offered this advice: "Don't get frustrated when you come across a passage that you cannot understand. Keep reading and God will give you what you need to know at that time."

In the weeks that followed I immersed myself in the reading of Scripture. Never before had God been so close and so real. With tears of joy streaming down my face I flushed my supply of marijuana down the toilet and discarded my pipes, rolling paper, and other related paraphernalia. From the time that the cross stopped smiling until the night my piano teacher reintroduced me to Jesus, God had been patiently, lovingly, relentlessly pursuing me. Now as never before I was in pursuit of God. My life after God was underway.

Life after God is different for each of us. In every instance the details of our relationship with Jesus Christ coalesce perfectly with the contours of our own respective stories. There is no such thing as one-size-fits-all Christianity. To say that a person's spiritual journey is deficient because it lacks a detail from our own story that we happen to hold in high esteem is to ignore the genius of a God who delights in endless variety. God meets every person in the living of his or her life. God and we, in fact, have never had separate journeys, as the Psalmist says so well:

O LORD, you have searched me and you know me.
    You know when I sit and when I rise;
    you perceive my thoughts from afar.
You discern my going out and my lying down;
    you are familiar with all my ways.
Before a word is on my tongue
    you know it completely, O LORD.
    Where can I go from your Spirit?
Where can I flee from your presence?
If I go up to the heavens, you are there;
    if I make my bed in the depths, you are there.

If I rise on the wings of the dawn,
　　if I settle on the far side of the sea,
　　even there your hand will guide me,
　　your right hand will hold me fast.
My frame was not hidden from you
　　when I was made in the secret place.
When I was woven together in the depths of the earth,
　　your eyes saw my unformed body.
All the days ordained for me
　　were written in your book
　　before one of them came to be.
When I awake, I am still with you.

　　　　　　　　　　　　(Psalm 139:1–4, 7–10, 15, 16, 18b)

Each of us has what we may call "salvific experiences," awakenings, when we find ourselves anew in God's embrace. The New Testament concept of "salvation" is best understood in this vein rather than as an unrepeatable *magic moment.* And hopefully these recurring experiences are happy events. Philosopher Søren Kierkegaard prayed as much: "Father in Heaven. When the thought of thee wakes in our hearts, let it not awaken like a frightened bird that flies about in dismay, but like a child waking from its sleep with a heavenly smile."[3] That is my prayer in writing this book. May every awakening to God's presence fill your soul with peace and joy.

2. Messy Spirituality

When I want to do good, evil is right there with me. For in my inner being I delight in God's law; but I see another law at work in the members of my body, waging war against the law of my mind and making me a prisoner of the law of sin at work within my members.

Romans 7:21–23

For as long as I can remember, I have wanted to be a godly person. Yet when I look at the yesterdays of my life, what I see, mostly, is a broken, irregular path littered with mistakes and failure. I have had temporary successes and isolated moments of closeness to God, but I long for the continuing presence of Jesus. Most of the moments of my life seem hopelessly tangled in a web of obligations and distractions.

Mike Yaconelli, *Messy Spirituality*

Predictable Unpredictability

The title of this chapter is shamelessly borrowed from Mike Yaconelli's book, *Messy Spirituality*. No other expression captures with greater simplicity or sophistication the stark reality of life in Christ. After years of service as a pastor and seminary professor, I feel sufficiently qualified to say that our individual faith journeys have one thing in common. Irrespective of our diverse life experiences, religious traditions, and individual circumstances – whether we pinpoint a decisive "conversion experience" when at once we were freed from our depraved estate, or we construe life in Christ as a continuing series of events from infancy to the present – our journeys are similarly *alternating* and *undulating*.

We gain ground and lose ground. We sin. We repent. Our faith seems to grow then shrink; flag then flourish. The journey is seriously deflated and steadily plodding; hopelessly doused yet unquenchably ignited. Around-and-round and up-and-down, the process of spiritual growth is precisely this: *There is no predictable process of spiritual growth.* The faith journey is as unpredictable as life itself.

If we dare to be honest with ourselves – and each other – we would admit that our relationship with Christ brings no silver bullet, no magic potion, no set of self-imposed habits (in clusters of three, five, seven, or twelve) by which we achieve a given benchmark of spiritual stability or happiness. What makes our individual faith journeys so similar is, in a word, their *messiness*.

Messiness would certainly be the right way to describe my faith journey. No sooner had my newfound pursuit of God begun than life at home took a serious downturn. My all-consuming love for Christ evoked a fanaticism that both stunned and worried my parents. To make matters worse, I started to repeat the "anti-Mary" sentiments expressed by Merriam, my piano teacher who had recently introduced me to an entirely unknown dimension of God's love.

My mother reminded me that she had had five miscarriages before I was born, that she had almost lost me in her fifth month of pregnancy, *and would have* – she said – had it not been for the Novena to the Blessed Mother, in which she, like Samuel's mother, Hannah, dedicated me to God.[1] That I would now consider such prayer idolatrous was devastating to my mother. As time went on I became more anti-Catholic in my views, which ultimately brought an end to the decades-long friendship between my mother and Merriam. I severed my ties with the Roman Catholic Church and started attending a Protestant church. Tensions at home reached their zenith when my sister, Colleen, chose to follow my example and leave the Catholic Church. At that point, I found a roommate and moved into my own place, never again to live at home. Fifteen years would pass before my parents and I could have a civil conversation about spiritual matters.

To say that I left Roman Catholicism in favor of Protestantism is to grossly oversimplify the matter. The transition from one traditional stream to another, and the journey that ensued, has been anything but smooth and predictable. There have been times of falling back into old habits and falling forward into new ones, which proved just as bad. I have enjoyed seasons of delight and endured dark nights of the soul – some of which I will touch on throughout the balance of this book. Sometimes I have loved Christians; at other times I have wished that Jesus never conceived of the church.

Mike Yaconelli describes the chaotic, unsteady nature of our spiritual lives in prose whose universality rivals that of the best Hallmark cards:

> My life is a mess.
>
> After forty-five years of trying to follow Jesus, I keep losing him in the crowded busyness of my life. I know Jesus is there somewhere, but it's difficult to make him out in the haze of everyday life.[2]

The Law of Undulation

In his well-loved novel, *The Screwtape Letters*, C. S. Lewis artfully depicted this strenuous mystery of human spirituality. A written exchange occurs between Lewis's characters "Screwtape," a senior demon, and his apprentice nephew, "Wormwood." Screwtape makes the following observation about human beings:

> Has no one ever told you about the Law of Undulation? Humans are amphibians – half spirit and half animal . . . This means that while their spirits can be directed to an eternal object, their bodies, passions, and imaginations are in continual change, for to be in time means to change. Their nearest approach to constancy, therefore, is undulation – the repeated return to a level from which they repeatedly fall back, a series of troughs and peaks.[3]

Scripture attests to this mystery of conflicting natures. Even if New Testament scholars have differing opinions about how the seventh chapter of St. Paul's epistle to the Romans should be interpreted, most Christians who read this passage find it difficult if not impossible *not* to resonate with this ostensibly autobiographical portrayal of undulating spirituality:

> I find this law at work: Although I want to do good, evil is right there with me. For in my inner being I delight in God's law; but I see another law at work in me, making me a prisoner of the law of sin at work within me. What a wretched man I am! Who will rescue me from this body of death? Thanks be to God, who delivers me through Jesus Christ our Lord. (Romans 7:21–25a, TNIV)

Elsewhere the Apostle Paul casts this in even plainer terms: "The sinful nature [literally, *the flesh*] desires what is contrary to the Spirit, and the Spirit what is contrary to the sinful nature. *They are in conflict with each other, so that you do not do what you want*" (Galatians 5:17, my emphasis). In this instance, Paul is clearly speaking of our experience as Christians. Sin, we might say, has been dethroned in the Christian's life, but not as of yet completely destroyed.

Cheap Grace versus Costly Grace

If we do not take this law of undulation into account when we consider Scripture's many admonitions to excel in the things of the Spirit, we set ourselves up for untold complications in the Christian life. We develop distorted and unrealistic expectations of ourselves and each other, and we fall into the either–or trap of settling for (what we are led to believe is) "cheap grace" or engaging in the dogged pursuit of the perfect, "sanctified life."

The term "cheap grace" was popularized by German theologian, Dietrich Bonhoeffer, who contrasted it with "costly grace." According to Bonhoeffer, cheap grace "is the grace we bestow on ourselves . . . grace without discipleship." It is "the preaching of forgiveness without requiring repentance, baptism without church discipline, Communion without confession, absolution without personal confession . . . it is grace without the cross, grace without Jesus Christ, living and incarnate." "Costly grace," by contrast, is nothing less than "the gospel which must be sought again and again, the gift which must be asked for, the door at which a man must knock." Such grace is costly, says Bonhoeffer, "because it costs a man his life, and it is grace because it gives a man the only true life."[4]

Some popular descriptions of cheap grace and costly grace have created much confusion among followers of Christ by omitting Bonhoeffer's insightful "again-and-again" theme from the latter category. Bonhoeffer plainly acknowledged the undulating character of Christian spirituality. Costly grace, he said, brings us back, "again and again," to seek the gift of reconciliation in Christ. And Bonhoeffer recognized that it is nothing less than grace, rightfully understood and internalized, that impels us to return to Christ in every instance of failure, and to die, again and again, to the one who alone gives us life. To miss this basic assumption of undulating spirituality in Bonhoeffer's depiction of costly grace is to miss the New Testament's emphasis on grace as the Christian's chief motivator in overcoming the power of sin and living into the call of discipleship.

The New Testament contains dozens of passages by a variety of apostolic writers that challenge us to improve our spiritual condition. But a careful reading of these texts also reveals the dynamic interplay between the law of undulation, which is at work in our conflicted spiritual selves, and costly grace, which draws us back again and again to the One in whom we live and move and have our being.

In John's Gospel, for example, Jesus admonished his followers to remain in him, for only in this way can one bear fruit: "No branch can bear fruit by itself; it must remain in the vine. Neither can you bear fruit unless you remain in me" (John 15:4). Bearing fruit does not result from *doing*; it results from *remaining*. And what's more, Jesus says that when we remain in him, he remains in us. The Source of abundant fruit bearing, in other words, is Jesus, not us (15:5).

Jesus' image of fruit-bearing branches that draw life from
the vine means something other than evangelistic duplication
or good works, as some interpreters suggest. It conveys the
message that we are uniquely gifted human beings in a life-
sustaining relationship with the risen Christ, the true vine.
Just as engrafted branches bear fruit after their own kind,
so human beings grafted to Christ bear fruit in a manner
consistent with their God-given nature and calling.

Picture a tree to which the branches of other fruit-bearing
trees have been grafted. When I was a boy I saw such a tree
in my Uncle Kenny's backyard. I was amazed to discover
that while the tree gave life to the branches, the branches
for their part continued to bear the fruit that was in their
nature to bear. When we remain in Christ, the vine, we bear
whatever fruit we were created to bear – and Scripture attests
to the fact that our fruit, of necessity, is not the same (see 1
Corinthians 12:21–27).[5]

In another New Testament passage, the Apostle Peter lists
seven virtues (not "habits," "principles," or "steps," mind
you) that are to characterize our lives as disciples (goodness,
knowledge, self-control, perseverance, godliness, mutual
affection, and love), along with the following assurance: "If
you possess these qualities in *increasing measure*, they will
keep you from being ineffective and unproductive in your
knowledge of our Lord Jesus Christ" (2 Peter 1:5–8, my
emphasis).

To take this verse by itself could leave us with the
impression that Peter envisioned our spiritual journey as a
steady, unbroken ascent toward Christlikeness. However, the
next sentence demonstrates Peter's awareness that another
scenario may just as likely occur: "But if any of you do not
have these virtues, you are nearsighted and blind, and have
forgotten that you have been cleansed from your past sins"
(1:9). One sentence later Peter explains why he is writing
such things: "So I will always remind you of these things,
even though you know them and are firmly established in
the truth you now have" (1:12).

It is important that we not miss the twin themes of
undulation and costly grace in this passage. Peter suggests

that upward spiritual progress in the Christian life arises out
of the continual awareness of God's mercy and grace. The
cycle of undulation takes its downward turn at the precise
moment we become spiritually inattentive to God's grace
and forget the cleansing of past sin.

The Apostle Paul makes a similar point in several places.
In 1 Thessalonians, which many New Testament scholars
believe to be Paul's first canonical letter, Paul urges disciples
on to ever-increasing growth: "As for other matters, brothers
and sisters, we instructed you how to live in order to please
God, as in fact you are living. *Now we ask you and urge you
in the Lord Jesus to do this more and more*" (1 Thessalonians
4:1, TNIV, my emphasis). But at the end of this epistle, after a
series of urgings and admonitions to rise above our fleshly
impulses, Paul offers up a doxology with this as its closing
statement: "The one who calls you is faithful and he will do
it" (5:24, TNIV).

St. Paul likewise exhorted the Christians at Colossae: "So
then, just as you received Christ Jesus as Lord, continue to
live your lives in him, *rooted* and *built up* in him, *strengthened*
in the faith as you were taught, and *overflowing with
thankfulness*" (Colossians 2:6, 7, TNIV, my emphasis). Paul
warns that we mustn't try to reverse the spiritual downturns
of the law of undulation through the dogged pursuit of
Christian perfection. He sounds the theme of costly grace
loudly and clearly, declaring that we have died to "the basic
principles of this world" and are therefore no longer subject
to such graceless rules as, "Do not handle! Do not Taste!
Do not touch!" While these kinds of regulations have "an
appearance of wisdom" to the ill-informed, they are actually
of no value "in restraining sensual indulgence" (2:20–23, TNIV).
Instead, since we "have been raised with Christ," we are to
set our hearts "on things above, where Christ is seated at the
right hand of God," and thereby "put to death" whatever still
belongs to our "earthly nature," such as "sexual immorality,
impurity, lust, evil desires and greed, which is idolatry"
(3:1–5, TNIV).

Paul was confident that the One who began a good work
in us would "carry it on to completion until the day of

Christ Jesus" (Philippians 1:6, my emphasis), and he offered the following prayer for disciples everywhere:

> I pray that out of his glorious riches [God] may strengthen you with power through his Spirit in your inner being, so that Christ may dwell in your hearts through faith. And I pray that you, being rooted and established in love, may have power, together with all the saints, to grasp how wide and long and high and deep is the love of Christ, and to know this love that surpasses knowledge – *that you may be filled to the measure of all the fullness of God*" (Ephesians 3:16–19, TNIV, my emphasis).[6]

This last passage underscores an important fact: being filled to "the measure of all the fullness of God" comes through our experience of Christ's love, which surpasses or transcends human knowledge.

This experience takes place – as we see in Ephesians 4:9–16 – within the relational interdependency that exists in Christian community. The risen Christ established apostolic leadership in the church for this very purpose – "to equip God's people for works of service, so that the body of Christ may be built up until we all reach *unity in the faith* and in the knowledge of the Son of God and *become mature, attaining to the whole measure of the fullness of Christ.*" "From him," Paul says, "the whole body, *joined and held together by every supporting ligament*, grows and builds itself up *in love*, as each part does its work" (4:12, 16, TNIV).[7]

What is most important to note from this brief survey of biblical texts is that we are called, in view of God's costly grace, to rise to greater spiritual heights, in the context of a faith journey that is consistently inconsistent, alternating and undulating – a journey that is, in a word, messy. To gloss over this stark reality of the Christian life is to open the door to untold sorrows – the subject of the next chapter.

3. Perils of Sin Management

Those who live according to the sinful nature have their minds set on what that nature desires; but those who live in accordance with the Spirit have their minds set on what the Spirit desires.
Romans 8:5

Jesus spent a disproportionate amount of time with people described in the gospels as: the poor, the blind, the lame, the lepers, the hungry, sinners, prostitutes, tax collectors, the persecuted, the downtrodden, the captives, those possessed by unclean spirits, all who labor and are heavy burdened, the rabble who know nothing of the law, the crowds, the little ones, the least, the last, and the lost sheep of the house of Israel. In short, Jesus hung out with ragamuffins.
Brennan Manning, *The Ragamuffin Gospel*

Hurray for Ragamuffins

My disordered faith journey has brought me to a place of renewed appreciation for the Roman Catholic Church, which formed me in ways that time has proved to be most spiritually beneficial. All the Catholic Church's bad press aside, Protestantism has little if any claim to the moral high ground. It matters not whether we are Catholic Christians or Protestant Christians – we are individually and collectively, in Brennan Manning's words, nothing more than *Ragamuffins*.[1] This is true whether we believe it or not. To refuse to accept this odious fact about ourselves is, if we are to accept Scripture's word on the matter, to court the worst kind of self-deception: "If we claim to be without sin, we deceive ourselves and the truth is not in us" (1 John 1:8).

Whether Catholic or Protestant, however, our reluctance to embrace our ragamuffin identity is rooted in something more elusive than mere self-deception. The problem with many of us is twofold: we are ashamedly aware of our depravity and we are deathly afraid to expose such ugliness to our fellow disciples. The reason behind this sad conundrum is even more scandalous. In many instances, it is our own faith communities – our churches – that have socialized us to believe and behave as posers. "We are, after all, *Christians*."

Unhealthy Preoccupation with Sin

In my study of theology I have discovered that Protestantism offers little more than Catholicism in vouchsafing confidence that God loves us – even *likes us* – in this undulating, ragamuffin state of ours. Protestant theology is complex, to be sure, but it tends to ride along two main tracks. The first emphasizes the theme of "eternal security," captured well in the popular phrase, "once saved, always saved." In this system, God alone is sovereign in salvation – through grace he draws us to himself and infuses us with the capacity to believe, and thus receive, his gift of salvation in Christ.

The second theological track stresses the role of human free will. In this scheme, God holds out the offer to accept or reject the gift of salvation in Christ. This offer is available to all human beings, who have the capacity at will to believe or disbelieve the gospel. After a person embraces Jesus Christ, he or she retains the freedom to reject this gift at any time.

Both traditions rightly stress God's goodness and benevolence. Both highlight the central role of Jesus Christ in securing and sustaining human salvation. But, at face value at least, one would think the once-saved-always-saved position would infuse a greater sense of security in our relationship with Christ. Ironically this is often not the case at all.

Not unlike the quandary I found myself in as a Roman Catholic youth – fearing that my sins made for a mortal rift between God and me – Protestants in both camps are left to wonder whether their sins are not, in the end, their undoing. In the once-saved-always-saved camp, the logic goes something like this. Scripture says that we draw the assurance of being rightly related to God through our faithful obedience to his commands:

> We know that we have come to know him if we obey his commands. Those who say, "I know him," but do not do what he commands are liars, and the truth is not in them. But if anyone obeys his word, love for God is truly made complete in them. This is how we know we are in him: Whoever claims to live in him must live as Jesus did. (1 John 2:3–5, TNIV)

Admittedly this is a tall order. Moreover, it raises the same type of venial-sin/mortal-sin dilemma that many Catholics encounter: At what point does our failure to obey God's commands constitute sufficient evidence that we are *not* the children of God we claim to be? Alternatively, when can we honestly say to our own satisfaction that we are "living as Jesus lived?" Here the once-saved-always-saved proposal turns in on itself. If our walk does not match our talk, then we may not in truth be what we suppose ourselves to be – *we are not really Christians at all*. Theologians of this stripe have their answers, of course, but at a visceral level even they labor under the law of undulation.

In the freewill camp everything is up for grabs. I attended a college that was steeped in this tradition. One day in class the professor shared what he hoped would be a thought-provoking parable. A Christian man was driving his car down the highway one day when he came upon a car that was traveling very slowly – far below the speed limit. "What's up with this?" the man growled to himself. It was a clear day and the road conditions were ideal. As he got closer, he noticed that the vehicle in front of him was piloted by an elderly lady whose nose barely cleared the dashboard. They crawled at the same, slow pace for what seemed an interminable period of time with no passing lane in sight.

This was the man's pet peeve – getting stuck behind incompetent motorists that had no business carrying a driver's license. Like a caldron of boiling oil he began to seethe with anger. Hatred toward this doddering old woman – and all other drivers like her – pressed into his intestines with unbearable force. He erupted in a towering rage, hurling profane insults at the woman, who remained oblivious to the fact that she was being tailgated. He had all he could stand. Taking the Lord's name in vain, the crazed man stomped the accelerator to the floorboard and wheeled his car across the double-yellow line to pass. In that moment a semi truck appeared out of the blind curve and hit the man's car head on, killing him instantly.

With the situational stage sufficiently set, the professor probed, "This man was a Christian. He attended church faithfully and was actively engaged in community service. He was a faithful husband and a doting father. But he died in a state that was anything but Christian. He was in an ugly, profane rage that drove him to hatred and recklessness. So here's the question: Was this man saved when he died?" The first students to respond represented the majority view. They alleged that the man had died in a state of perdition. Sadly, he had fallen from grace in the final moments of his life.

The lesson of the day, ironically, was on the security we enjoy in our relationship with Christ. The professor went on to assure us that it is not the onetime, out-of-character sins that break our relationship with Christ, but rather one's general tenor of life. In the case of the fallen driver, we can be confident that his soul ascended to the welcoming arms of Christ. The professor then directed us to 1 John 1:5–7:

> This is the message we have heard from him and declare to you: God is light; in him there is no darkness at all. If we claim to have fellowship with him yet walk in the darkness, we lie and do not live by the truth. But if we walk in the light, as he is in the light, we have fellowship with one another, and the blood of Jesus, his Son, purifies us from all sin.

He went on to observe: "This passage says that if we 'walk in the light' the blood of Jesus purifies us from all sin. Correct?" Reasonably certain this was not a trick question we answered, "Yes, the text appears to be saying that." The skillful instructor continued, "In this passage when John says 'all sin,' what sin is he talking about? The class was silent. After a pregnant pause he answered his own question: "*It is the sin that we commit while we walk in the light.*"

It took awhile for the point of this profound theological observation to sink in, but eventually we all got it. "Walking in the light" does not describe sinless perfection. As verse 8 goes on to say, we deceive ourselves to think that we do not commit sin. In the context of this passage, walking in the light means living life in relationship with Jesus Christ. Yes, we have ups and downs and sin does in fact occur. But we need not worry, because – the professor citing the nuance of the original language – "the blood of Jesus *continually cleanses* us from all sin."

I have no doubt that this professor's take on the matter is correct, and I have repeated this observation (minus the crazy driver story) to my students and fellow parishioners for many years. Still we must acknowledge the inadequacy of a system that grounds a relationship with God on our success in managing personal sin. The freewill group tends to be no less tormented by the law of undulation. If it is the "general tenor of life" that defines whether or not we are walking in the light, and our tenor of life is anything but "general" and "thematic," at what point do we begin to doubt that we are walking in the light at all? When we reach the lowest points of undulation, it seems that darkness is all there is. Now back to my claim that the church socializes us into believing and behaving as posers.

Church: A Scary Place for Sinners

Put plainly, many of us do not consider church to be a safe place to deal with basic life issues, much less our degeneracy. We recoil at the thought that people at church would find out that we have a drinking problem, a gambling addiction, or a drug habit. There's no way we would tell them about the pornographic websites we've viewed recently or the jealous thoughts we harbor toward that nice-looking woman at church to whom we suspect our husband has taken a liking. We would never turn to the church for help in getting out of the affair we're having with our coworker or in dealing with our abusive spouse. We may know that we have anger management issues, but we certainly wouldn't turn to anybody at church for guidance. Imagine what the people at church would think if they found out that I was molesting my foster daughter or that my wife and I were frequenting spouse-swapping parties. And if you're a leader at church, the stakes are even higher. You would rather lose an index finger than undergo the disgrace of having your church find about your sordid private life.

You ask if church people do such things. Every one of these examples is taken from the lives of real, churchgoing Christians with whom I have been associated over the last three decades. To be sure, the list of examples and variety of sins is much more extensive than that. I will refrain from saying more than I should about the visit I paid to a pastor several years ago. The secretary was not at her desk so I made my way to the pastor's office, which was located at the back of the sanctuary. The door was closed when I approached, so I knocked three times and made my entry. As I came in the pastor sat up behind his desk – wide-eyed and erect, staring straight at me. Assuming I had his full attention I began to explain the reason for my visit. Just then a rustling noise behind the desk stopped me in mid sentence. Perceiving that I had heard something, the pastor looked down by his side and acted surprised to find the church secretary crouched in the small space between his desk and bookshelf. "I was looking for a pencil," she said with flushed red cheeks. A pencil indeed!

Community Building versus Sin Management

The rehearsal of this dark side of our Christian existence drives me to consider the observations made by theologians James Wm. McClendon, Jr. and Ray S. Anderson. Both in their own ways have stressed that theological reflection, in its best form, is the analysis of the church's concrete practices (McClendon calls these "powerful practices"). Basic to all churchly practice is the communal formation of the church itself. That is to say, the church's primary practice is *being the church*. Church" in the original language of the New Testament is "assembly" – *ekklesia* – the *gathered community* of disciples. The building of relationships in community, therefore, is the church's most basic powerful practice, and therefore the principal subject of theological reflection. And the guiding question of such theological reflection is this: *How well is the church doing in terms of fostering authentic, Christ-focused, mutually edifying community?*

My friend, Leonard Sweet, doesn't believe that the church is doing what it should in its community-building practices. He pointed out in a recent conversation that the church is no longer – if it ever was – looked to as a "relationship expert." Today, he says, if people are grappling with life or relationship issues, they seek out the advice of a Dr. Phil, an Oprah, a Dr. Laura, or a Delilah.

A Case of Cat-and-Mouse Spirituality

Christian philosopher, Dallas Willard, appears to have put his finger on why the church is often not the place to find the healthiest of relationships. He says that the church's main preoccupation throughout the last one hundred years or so has been what he terms "sin management."[2] The underlying rationale of the sin-management mentality is this: focus all present efforts on the eradication of sin so that we will go to heaven when we die. Almost no attention, says Willard, is given to living the eternal-kind of life *now*.

In its current preoccupation with sin, the church has inadvertently empowered the very thing it intended to manage. It has become the taboo that we dare talk about only in the abstract. We may speak of concrete instances of sin in other people's lives, but seldom are we willing to name it and claim it openly in our own lives. It is much more comfortable at church to pretend that all is well in our

world. And in our refusal to confront the corrosive presence
of sin in our lives, we deprive one another of the chance to
be the church that Jesus dreamed of before the world was
created.[3]

The truth is that we do realize some success in managing
sin – when our undulating spirituality is at its peak. But,
assuming an equal distribution of peaks and troughs, these
peak times encompass about 25 percent of the journey at
best. The rest of the time we're either descending into a
trough, traveling through the trough, or heading toward
another peak. In practical terms, this means that 75 percent
of the time we are only pretending to have it together. Those
engaged in sin-management spirituality act like they have
the upper hand on sin, and they may do a pretty good job
convincing others (and even themselves) that this is the case,
but more often than not, it simply is not so.

Feigning spiritual health has become the received social
norm in the majority of Western churches. And we have
come up with a host of good things to fill the void of façade-
stripping community – things like Sunday school classes
and home Bible studies where we bolster our knowledge of
things spiritual; personal quiet times and powerful corporate
worship experiences that move us emotionally. Mind you,
growing in spiritual knowledge and affection is vitally
important, but it cannot stand as a substitute for the fostering
of healthy, transparent community that embraces its own in
all of their brokenness.

Distractions, Digressions, and Disasters

When a church is preoccupied with sin-management
spirituality, it is easy to major in minors and become woefully
sidetracked by trivial matters. One such experience is
particularly noteworthy. It occurred on a hot Sunday morning
in July 1984. Our church was located in a beach community
of southern California. Weeks earlier the congregation had
hosted a youth puppeteer group from Texas, which came out
to assist the church with its annual Vacation Bible School.

One of the teenaged girls stayed at an elder's house. She mentioned offhandedly in one of their conversations how much freer the dress code was in California. "The elders back home would *never* let us wear shorts to church," she remarked. The comment set off a firestorm on the elder board.

Against the strong objections of the pastoral staff, the elders concluded that shorts were "inappropriate attire" and that a decree saying as much would be presented to the church forthwith. One of the elders read the edict during announcement time: "*Upon much prayer and discussion, we the elders have determined that shorts are inappropriate attire for worship services and therefore enjoin the members not to wear such clothing to church from this point forward. Thank you.*"

I counted no less than a dozen visitors that morning who were wearing shorts. After the service ended, some of the half-naked guests bolted for the doors. Others slinked through the crowd, wishing quietly to dematerialize and vanish painlessly from sight. I was able to catch a few before they escaped. To a person they felt embarrassed and publicly dressed down in more ways than one. I apologized that they had to be there when the elders felt it necessary to take care of this housekeeping matter. All were gracious to my face, but none ever returned to the church.

I made a note to myself that day: "The risen Christ will remove this church's lampstand for this." The church gathered amid a culture that considered shorts to be perfectly acceptable casual wear for almost any occasion. That announcement marked a fundamental choice in terms of the direction the leaders wanted to go – a choice to do church in a manner that was soothing to their sin-management sensibilities but culturally disengaged. They were willing to sacrifice their witness to the community in order to conform to a standard of dress that was fifteen hundred miles removed. I left the beach-community church six years later to assume a senior pastoral role in another denomination. Not long afterward the leaders of the congregation, threatened by dwindling attendance and financial insolvency, sold the property to the Jehovah's Witnesses and merged with a sister congregation several miles inland. Their lampstand in the community was gone.[4] Sin-management spirituality had taken its ultimate toll.

More often, however, sin-management spirituality is evident in subtler ways – particularly in the way we treat those who are caught in sin. The story of Bobby Scott is a case in point. The church I served after moving from the beach community had a one-of-a-kind worship leader. He was a recovering alcoholic who could make the piano itself dance Kentucky Blue Grass. He would routinely transform the most insipid hymns into foot-stomping, hand-clapping choruses that gave Sunday morning worship the look and feel of a country hoedown. He also practiced an open-door policy in the recruitment of fellow musicians – a policy that drew a very gifted non-Christian musician, named Bobby Scott, into the orb of his ministry.

Bobby was a delightful individual with a winsome personality and seemingly unlimited musical talent. He played the guitar, mandolin, drums, trumpet, piano, and organ. He was an excellent vocalist and prolific songwriter. He also had an unfaithful wife.

Bobby professed faith in Jesus Christ not long after he started participating in the worship services. At the same time things in his marriage went from bad to worse. His wife became pregnant by the man she was cheating with and soon divorced Bobby and moved in with the father of the child. When the baby was born, she convinced the family court judge to stick Bobby with the child-support payments. He was devastated – and had it not been for the love and support he received from his friends at church, he would have been suicidal. Bobby steered clear of another relationship for nearly a year. Then, with wounds sufficiently healed, he found himself in love again. But this time, rather than leaving himself vulnerable to another vicious divorce, Bobby chose to abandon marriage and simply cohabit with his girlfriend.

When reports of Bobby's new living arrangement reached the elder board, it stirred no small conversation among the leaders of the church. Surely this sort of thing could not be tolerated, one elder intoned. Others agreed. Finally after much discussion the board appointed the elder in charge of worship ministries to contact Bobby to see if the rumors were true, and, if so, to "encourage him." I consider this one of the more memorable lapses in my pastoral leadership. With PhD studies looming and several ministerial duties pressing, I agreed to this decision and we moved on to the meeting's next agenda item.

A few days later the elder called Bobby on the phone. "Hello, Bobby? John Seymour here. Say, maybe you can clear up a rumor. We heard that you're living with your girlfriend . . . is that true?"

Shocked by the abruptness with which this near stranger broached the subject, Bobby answered the question with corresponding directness. "Yes, it's true. I'm living with my girlfriend. But I don't see what business that is of yours. What I do in my private life is not your concern."

Mr. Seymour was not known for his tact or gentleness in such situations. "That's where you're wrong, Bobby," he rejoined. "I'm sorry you feel that way but the fact is when you stand before the congregation and direct us in worship, you are exercising spiritual leadership. If you are engaged in an immoral relationship with your girlfriend, you have two choices: either move into separate homes and stop having sex, or excuse yourself from the worship team. I hate to be the bearer of bad news, but that's just the way it is." Mr. Seymour urged Bobby to reconsider his living arrangements and ended the conversation as abruptly as he had started it.

Bobby came to my office a few days later. As he walked through the door and sat down on the couch it was obvious that he was upset. Surmising that Mr. Seymour had something to do with his agitated state, I closed the door and sat on the adjoining chair. "How's it going, Bobby?" I inquired, smiling. Bobby turned to speak. Before he said a word I could read his face. It wasn't simple anger I saw. He was completely dispirited. In biblical terms, his countenance had fallen.

Bobby steeled himself and spoke slowly and deliberately. "I wanted to say this to your face. John Seymour called me *on the phone* to tell me that people have been talking behind

my back about my girlfriend and me." At that point I tried
to assure him that the matter had been handled much more
discreetly than that. But he held up his hand, signaling that
he wanted to finish what he started. "My wife began cheating
on me after the first year of our marriage. I sweat blood and
tears trying to make it work . . . *she ripped my heart out, man!*"
He cupped his face with both hands and started to weep. I
waited silently for him to collect himself and continue. "I'm
paying child support for a kid that's not even mine. I finally
found somebody I love, but I will never marry her. I can't.
I won't put myself in that position again. And now I am
told that what I do in my private life makes me an unfit
Christian." Again I tried to interject, and again he held me
off. "I don't have a problem with you, Pastor Chuck. But
Seymour didn't even have the decency to talk to me about
this to my face. He did his dirty work over the phone. That
doesn't seem like a very Christian way to handle something
like this. The bottom line is that I don't have to justify my
behavior to him or to you or to anybody else at this church.
I'm finished. I will never come back to this church again –
and there's nothing you can say to change my mind."

Believe me, I tried. We continued in cordial conversation
for about a half hour, but I could make no headway. The
damage was irreparable. As of the writing of these pages,
it has been eleven years since that conversation, and to my
knowledge Bobby has never returned to that (or to any other)
church.

In his attempt to "manage sin," Mr. Seymour set out to
attack an impersonalized problem rather than reach out to
an invaluable soul. To this day I regret that I did not neglect
some matters of lesser importance to deal with this myself.
In my mind I've walked through the encounter a hundred
times. I would invite Bobby to join me for a cup of coffee at
his favorite coffeehouse. I would ask how things were going
in his life a year after his painful divorce. I would listen.
If he broached the subject of his new girlfriend, I would
celebrate his finding of new love. I would dream with him
about the future. I would, in short, earn the right to talk
to him as a friend and spiritual guide. Only God knows if

the outcome would have been different. But this experience serves as a lasting and painful reminder of the perils of sin management.

Sometimes it gets even worse. Sin-management spirituality does not always stop with the ill-treatment of those who get caught in sin. Occasionally it even drives us to mistreat the victims of other people's offenses. Mike Dobbs and his wife, Sandy, had been married for about a year when they started teaching the church's second-grade Sunday school class. Mike was a construction worker and Sandy taught physical education at the local high school. Mike in particular shined in his role as Sunday school teacher.

Sandy and Mike served together well in that position for almost a year. Then something happened with Sandy. To Mike's dismay Sandy announced that she didn't love him – she had never loved him. She told Mike that she had married him out of fear that she was getting older and running out of options. But now she had found her soul mate and would be moving in with him immediately. She had already initiated divorce proceedings and all Mike had to do was "cooperate."

Understandably this revelation ravaged Mike. At first he was numb. As the days passed, numbness gave way to fury intermingled with shame and grief. But there was still one good thing in his life that buoyed his spirit – a silver lining that framed his dark world with a glimmer of joy: his role as second-grade Sunday school teacher.

The Sunday after Sandy left him, Mike showed up at church several minutes early, carrying his white cardboard box filled with the morning's Sunday school materials. He strode across the parking lot toward the classrooms. His back was straight (no trace of slumping self-pity) and a smile brightened his face. Even though the distress of the preceding week had left dark circles under his eyes, there was an equally conspicuous gleam that signaled his happy anticipation of what the morning with his children would bring.

I didn't see Mike again until the end of the Sunday school hour. He was walking from the classroom toward his car on the far side of the parking lot. His back was slumped. His eyes were hollow. His face was expressionless. He was leaving without his white cardboard box. Sensing something was very wrong, I walked across the parking lot and intercepted Mike halfway between the classroom and his car. "Is everything okay?" I inquired. He answered in a voice that was as flat as his complexion was pallid. He said that two of the church's elders had paid a visit to his classroom at the end of the Sunday school hour and relieved him of his duties. They learned that morning of his wife's leaving and had just come out of a meeting in which they had discussed the matter at length with the entire board. The two men informed Mike that with his marriage in such crisis the elders could not be sure he was still fit to serve as a Sunday school teacher. They took the box from Mike's hands and thanked him for understanding their dilemma. "I feel like I've just been kicked in the gut," Mike said. "I can't believe they would take away the only thing that gave me a reason to live." With that, Mike got into his car and drove away from the church – never again to return.

No wonder we are so skittish about the skeletons in our closets. Who in his or her right mind would volunteer to become a casualty of sin-management spirituality? It is safer by far simply to wrestle privately with the shame and insecurity of sin and to reserve church for less threatening activities. Catholics may be correct in saying that Protestantism is comparatively impoverished when it comes to established practices of confession. However, neither Catholics nor Protestants offer community-building practices that directly confront the impoverishing effects of personal sin in a secure and supportive environment. Recovering our "relationship expertise" as gathered followers of Jesus Christ necessarily involves confessing our sins to each other and praying for one another so that we may be healed (James 5:16).

In the final analysis, church will only become a place of spiritual healing and transformation when we take the risk to make it the most dangerous place of all – a place where we can be fully, completely ourselves.

4. Spiders, Flames, and an Angry God

Who is a God like you, who pardons sin and forgives the trans-gression of the remnant of his inheritance? You do not stay angry forever but delight to show mercy. You will again have compassion on us; you will tread our sins underfoot and hurl all our iniquities into the depths of the sea.

Micah 7:18, 19

I'd been trying to live up to the standards of an utterly holy God who, I was so often reminded, could not tolerate even one whiff of sin. Hadn't He laid the sins of the whole world on His own Son on the cross, and then turned His face away? If that was true, I'd thought, then God's stomach must turn every time He even thought about me with all the secret sins and inconsistencies in my life.

Jeff VanVonderen, *Tired of Trying to Measure Up*

Sinners in the Hands of an Angry God

It is ironic that some of the greatest exemplars of the Christian life are best remembered for what is least characteristic of their overall contribution. Jonathan Edwards is a case in point. Arguably the most brilliant American theologian of all time, Edwards is best remembered for his famous (infamous?) sermon, "Sinners in the Hands of an Angry God."[1] The sermon is unforgettable for at least two reasons: its vivid imagery and its lacerating analysis of our spiritual dark side.

Edwards invoked metaphor and simile in an oratorical style that stands unsurpassed to the present time. The sermon casts the themes of God's holiness and human sinfulness in the starkest of contrasting images. "The bow of God's wrath is bent," declares Edwards, "and the arrow made ready on the string, and justice bends the arrow at your heart, and strains the bow, and it is nothing but the mere pleasure of God, and that of an angry God, without any promise or obligation at all, that keeps the arrow one moment from being made drunk with your blood." (By now the original auditors of the sermon were no doubt squirming in the pews.)

Judging the bow-and-arrow metaphor inadequate by itself to convey the utter degradation of our sinful estate, Edwards resorted to simile of arachnoscopic proportions:

> The God that holds you over the pit of hell, much as one holds a spider, or some loathsome insect over the fire, abhors you, and is dreadfully provoked: his wrath towards you burns like fire; he looks upon you as worthy of nothing else, but to be cast into the fire; he is of purer eyes than to bear to have you in his sight; you are ten thousand times more abominable in his eyes, than the most hateful venomous serpent is in ours.

And to make sure the members of his congregation did not imagine that their pastor was talking about the awful people outside the church, Edwards made it crystal clear for whom this message was intended: "There is no other reason to be given why you have not gone to hell, since you have sat here in the house of God, provoking his pure eyes by your sinful wicked manner of attending his solemn worship. Yea, there is nothing else that is to be given as a reason why you do not this very moment drop down into hell."

Pastor Edwards was speaking to his own people – and as he did so his words produced fear and conviction of the most agonizing magnitude. Those who witnessed the event said that Edwards's sermon provoked his listeners to cry and to wail so loudly that he was unable to finish. But the reverberations of that fateful message extended well beyond the boundaries of that church service held on a sultry day in Enfield, Connecticut, July 8, 1741. Edwards did not have the reputation of being a hellfire preacher, and he wasn't angry when he preached his famous sermon. Nevertheless,

"Sinners in the Hands of an Angry God" is considered to be the most influential sermon in American history – rivaled only in the last century by Martin Luther King, Jr.'s epoch-making speech, "I Have a Dream" – and is credited for lasting the cultural dye of the Great Awakening, a watershed in American religious history.[2]

While much more could be said about the Great Awakening and the role that revivalism has played in the formation of American religious thought, one key datum has had a lasting impact on the way many of us have come to think about ourselves and God: *We are sinners and God is angry with us.* The revivalism spawned by the Great Awakening has influenced the proclamation of the gospel in North America and beyond ever since. This twin theme – our despicable sinfulness and God's wrathful anger – has constituted the warp and woof of our theological cloth. Even though such a spin on evangelistic preaching seems virtuous enough, it has in fact become the modern church's most crippling distraction.

From Guilt to Shame

Author and speaker, Jeff VanVonderen, is the executive director of Spiritual Abuse Recovery Resources. He is also a refugee of sin-management spirituality. He has dedicated his life to rescuing people from the abusiveness of shame-based religion. VanVonderen points out the profound difference between "guilt," which, he says, "is like a spiritual nerve-response to sin, an emotional response to wrong behavior," and "shame," which "is the belief or mindset that something is wrong with you." When we adopt a shame-based way of looking at ourselves, it doesn't matter how often we "get it right" spiritually. Deep down, says VanVonderen, we still believe that something is very wrong with ourselves.[3] He describes the devastating affects of spiritual shame in very personal terms:

Living with that continuous sense of shame, I'd entered into a process that involved three steps: trying, trying harder, and trying my hardest. Did I say three steps? Actually, there were four: I gave up – or at least I switched the standards by which I was trying to measure myself. True, the alcohol and drugs could have killed me physically, but to be honest, even though I had been a Christian, I was already nearly dead inside.[4]

Revisiting the Dark Side: A Saga of Shame and Grace

VanVonderen's story bears striking resemblance to my own. Two years after I left the Roman Catholic Church and began my journey in Protestantism, I found myself well established in a local congregation that boasted of "speaking where the Bible speaks and remaining silent where the Bible is silent." They held the Bible in high esteem and adhered to a strict lifestyle, which by and large frowned on the use of tobacco and alcohol. Steve Hallaway, the associate pastor, had taken me under his wing and the two of us had become good friends. We spent hours every week studying Scripture. He taught me how to share the gospel with unbelievers and challenged me to do the unthinkable – to preach a sermon to the marines in boot camp at San Diego's Marine Corp Recruit Depot (MCRD), where our church hosted Sunday worship services.

Steve helped me prepare the message, which was based on 1 Peter 2:9: "But you are a chosen people, a royal priesthood, a holy nation, a people belonging to God, that you may declare the praises of him who called you out of darkness into his wonderful light." At that time I was using the 1901 edition of the American Standard Version, which uses the phrase "peculiar people" in place of the New International Version's less ambiguous, "a people belonging to God." Thus the title of my very first sermon: "A Peculiar People."

Steve walked me through the process of distilling the text's key idea. Then he helped me develop the sermon's main points and sub-points. He directed me to several good sources from which I was able to glean the sermon's supplemental materials. Finally, he assisted me in the crafting of the introduction and conclusion. All in all the experience of preparing my first sermon was, in a word, easy. Steve made it so. But he wasn't finished.

Once I got the message in its final written form, Steve walked me into the church's sanctuary. He switched on the lights. Then he turned on the microphone attached to the large, wooden pulpit at the front of the building. "Now you're going to deliver the sermon as though this sanctuary were full of people." Reluctantly I assumed my position behind the pulpit. It felt strange and intimidating to view the sanctuary from that angle. Our eyes met as he made one final adjustment to the microphone. He smiled at me and said something I will never forget: "I'm going to make a preacher out of you."

These words were Steve's own, to be sure, but they carried a force that transcended this otherwise simple exchange. It was as if Jesus himself were saying this to me. Jesus was making himself present to me in Steve's friendship. After a long, sleepless night in which I tossed and turned in endless, sweat-drenched anxiety, I drove to MCRD to preach my first sermon. On the way I prayed aloud in the car: "Oh God, I could *never* do this on a regular basis. It would kill me!" When I stood to preach, however, all nervousness dissipated and I preached – *really preached*. This was a highpoint in my undulating spirituality – a highpoint that would soon be followed by a debilitating trough.

That day I received high praises from Steve and the others at church. These accolades were among many that had come my way since I started attending the church. I was Steve's star disciple. Peers and superiors in the faith held me in high esteem. They considered me leadership material. (During this season I developed a lot of flexibility in my right arm patting myself on the back.) The division manager at the *Los Angeles Times* had taken similar notice. Before long he offered me a home-delivery agency. It was gratifying to know that I was one of the youngest persons to whom he had ever made such an offer. I accepted.

My new responsibilities at work drew me away from church – or at least they served to divide my allegiances as never before. Some days I worked twelve to sixteen hours, surviving on three or four hours of sleep. I was successful in this new endeavor and took pride in my accomplishments. I also noticed that this newfound success was taking its toll on my spiritual life. Frankly, I found myself less interested in things of the Spirit. My work had become fulfillment enough. Steve and I kept in touch, but there simply wasn't the time to meet as we had in the past.

Before long some old urges, which I thought were gone for good, started to surface. A month earlier my Christian roommate had moved out to be closer to San Diego State University where he was a student. I was on my own. One night I acted on a craving that had pestered me for two weeks – I stopped at a liquor store on my way home and picked up a twelve pack of beer. By the time I finished the sixth beer I was ready to smoke some marijuana. So I called a friend from the past. He was at my place in under an hour, and for the first time in two years I was smoking pot.

The next day I was overwhelmed with guilt and remorse. I called Steve and told him everything. But I wasn't prepared for his reaction. He was abrasive and (it seemed) judgmental. He did not sympathize in the least – he was *angry*. "I'm not a bit surprised," he said harshly. "You're right back in the same stinking pit that Jesus pulled you out of two years ago. I can't believe I spent all that time with you just to see this happen. What a waste. I'm disgusted with you." I told Steve that I was sorry and ended the conversation.

I felt hopeless and helpless. There was no other Christian friend to turn to. I was too ashamed to tell anyone else at church what had happened. If Steve was that disappointed about what I had done, what would the others think? At the same time I discovered that my old friends were more than happy to receive me back into their fold. Within a few short weeks I was in the full embrace of my old habits. It didn't take long for news of my falling away to run its course through the entire church.

For several months, with the exception of a phone call now and then from Fran, an elderly lady who kept track of attendance, I heard nothing from the people at church.

Eventually I moved into another apartment with Craig
Boudet, a friend I knew from high school who shared my
appetite for the party life. I was left to imagine what the folks
at church were saying about me: "I guess Chuck wasn't as
spiritual as he led us to believe." "Yeah Chuck talked a good
talk, but he obviously doesn't have what it takes for the long
haul." It made little difference whether such conversations
actually occurred. The shame was palpable.

Early one evening there was a knock at my door. Several
friends were gathering at my place for a marijuana party, so
I assumed that the knock signaled the arrival of more guests.
The festivities had in fact already begun and the apartment
was thick with the sweet, smooth aroma of Sinsemilla. I swung
the door open. A greeting for my pot-smoking buddies was
already rolling off my tongue. The faces of the three people
on my porch were familiar but out of place. They belonged
to the church's singles group, which was meeting that night
at a member's house just down the street. They had stopped
by to say hello.

We stood there looking at each other in mutual stunned
silence. Marijuana smoke wafted generously into their nostrils.
Then Mike Green, one of the three, stepped forward and
looked into my eyes with the unmistakable, uncontaminated
tenderness of Jesus. Without saying a word he embraced me.
His hug communicated an unconditionality that I had longed
for in my fellow Christians but had never before experienced.
Before he let go he whispered something that no one else
could hear: "We miss you, Chuck. We'll always love you,
no matter what. We want you back." I thanked them for
stopping by and we wished each other a good night. In that
spontaneous act of kindness, Mike had made himself one in
body and spirit with Jesus.

Several weeks passed and I could not forget Mike's short
visit. Jesus himself was calling me back. Every time I drove
past a church building I could hear Jesus beckoning me home.
Then something quite unexpected happened. My roommate,
Craig, was in love with a young woman named Jennifer
Stanford. Jennifer, for her part, wasn't so sure about Craig.
They had very little in common by Jennifer's reckoning.

She was contemplative. He was a pragmatist. She was an introvert who loved to read. He was an extrovert who loved to party. She was intrigued by questions of a spiritual nature. He was vehemently opposed to any such nonsense.

One morning Jennifer and I struck up a conversation. She had spent the night and Craig was at work. We had talked about spiritual matters in the past, but Craig's doleful stare always ensured that these exchanges were brief. "I've always considered myself a spiritual person," declared Jennifer. "But I think that everybody has to find their own way. What's good for one person might not be so good for another. 'Different strokes for different folks,' as they say." I sympathized with how Jennifer felt. I thought much the same thing during my long sojourn on the dark side. "But wait a minute," I reflected, "I'm back on the dark side too. I have been there now for about nine months. But I don't want to be there any longer. Jesus wants me back, and some of the people at church – at least Mike and a few others in the singles group – want me back too."

By this point Jennifer had fallen silent. I had let her comment about different strokes hang in the air beyond the socially acceptable limit. She gazed at me quizzically – waiting quietly for me to return from my thoughts. I took notice of my black, leather-bound Bible sitting on the table in the corner of the living room. A thick layer of dust gave it a grayish hue. I hadn't touched it in months. Bracing myself for what I would do next, I began to speak. "Jennifer . . . I know exactly what your heart is longing for. I would like to share something with you that changed my whole world. I know my life doesn't look any different right now. I've really gotten off track over the last several months." Then, double-checking my readiness to make such a commitment, I said, "But I'll make a deal with you. If you believe what I'm going to tell you about Jesus Christ and want to give your life to him, I promise that I will recommit myself to Christ and we will do this thing together. What do you say?" "It's a deal!" Jennifer exclaimed.

I wiped the dust from my Bible and grabbed a fresh pad of yellow paper from the kitchen counter. Jennifer and I moved to the dinning room table. I shared the gospel message just as Steve had taught me, illustrating the death, burial, and resurrection of Jesus on the paper. I explained that in the original language of the New Testament "gospel" literally means "good news." I pointed out that we can only appreciate how good this good news is when we understand how badly off we are without it. The bottom line, I told Jennifer, is that humanity has a sin problem that only Jesus can fix. I said much more, reading several passages from Scripture and making other notations on the yellow paper.

After I completed my presentation I asked Jennifer if she believed this message about Jesus and his saving work on the cross. She said she did. Then I asked if she wanted to give her life to Jesus Christ. Her eyes welled with tears. Nodding her head, her answer was barely audible. "Yes," she replied. I told her how happy I was about this decision and assured her that I would hold up my end of the bargain. I would return to the church I had attended and announce my intention to recommit my life to Christ.

That morning Jennifer and I drove to the church building with great anticipation. She wanted to be baptized on the spot . . . and she wanted me to baptize her. For my part, I was looking forward to telling the pastor and whoever else happened to be there that I was finally returning home to my church family where I belonged.

Three people greeted us when we arrived: Daniel Longerham, the senior pastor, Mary Sue Snider, the church secretary, and Melvin Lamm, one of the church's elders. They looked surprised but delighted to see us. I introduced Jennifer to the group and then Daniel invited us into his office. Jennifer and I sat next to each other on the leather couch in Pastor Longerham's spacious office, which doubled as the church library. Daniel pulled an armchair from the corner and positioned it right in front of us. He sat down and said, "I'm anxious to hear why you've come in today." I shared all that had happened in my life over the last nine months and the deal that Jennifer and I had made that morning. I told him that I wanted to rededicate myself to Jesus. Jennifer spoke up and said that she had just given her life to Christ and wanted me to baptize her. Daniel was overjoyed. "This is an answer to our prayers, Chuck. We've been praying for you ever since you left." He looked at Jennifer and said, "Jennifer, what can I say? You are making the best decision of your life. No other choice – including who you will marry – is as important as the decision to follow Jesus Christ. I think it's wonderful to have Chuck baptize you. Let's get you both ready."

Daniel opened his office door and announced the good news to Mary Sue and Melvin. The five of us excitedly made our way toward the front of the sanctuary where the baptistery and changing rooms were located. As we walked down the aisle Daniel briefed the others on who would be baptizing Jennifer. Then I noticed in the corner of my eye that Melvin was tugging on Daniel's shirtsleeve, trying to get his attention without anyone else noticing. The two stopped walking and Melvin leaned over to whisper something in Daniel's ear. Neither tact nor diplomacy was Melvin's middle name, so it didn't take much effort to hear what he said: "You're letting Chuck baptize Jennifer? He can't do that unless he's rededicated his life to Christ." Daniel assured him that I had in fact already done that. Melvin persisted, "Did you *pray* with him?" Sighing, Daniel answered, "Well . . . no." Melvin shook his head and held up both hands in a hold-everything kind of pose. He said in a voice loud enough for all to hear, "Chuck doesn't have any business baptizing this girl until he's restored."

Her mouth agape, Jennifer looked at me, wide eyed. Daniel broke the awkward silence. "Chuck, I know your heart, but I think it would be best for us to pray together for your rededication and restoration to the fellowship of Christ's church." "Hey, that's fine with me," I answered. "I'm glad to do whatever you think is necessary." We joined hands in a circle. Melvin prayed out first, thanking God for my desire to return to the fold and live my life for Christ. Daniel followed, expressing the same sentiments. I finished by prayerfully affirming – "in the presence of these brothers and sisters" – that I was in fact repentant and sincere in my desire to be right with Jesus Christ and his people." We then proceeded with Jennifer's baptism.

Several days later Daniel apologized for Melvin's behavior and asked if I was offended by this exchange. I assured him that I was not. It was nice to be back. That Daniel's question made me rethink what had happened that day – and in the years since then, the events surrounding my falling away and return have served as a subject of theological reflection concerning the church's unwitting vacillation between "shaming behavior" and "grace-giving behavior."

Accepting what we Are and Aren't

What I have tried to show thus far is that the fact of our Christian existence is one of *undulating spirituality*. Walking in the light, as Scripture attests, is a journey that includes recurring sin – not the "walking-in-darkness" sort of sin, which we could describe as wholesale rebellion against God and his ways, but recurring sin nonetheless. Ours is a messy spirituality. It will be so until our redemption in Christ is fulfilled in glory. Our amphibious nature – "half spirit and half animal" (C. S. Lewis) – dictates that we will visit and revisit the guilt of sin.

The problem, as I have observed in these first few chapters, is in how the church has typically dealt with this fact. Although there are notable exceptions, the church by and large adopted sin-management strategies that, ironically, empowered the very thing it sought to control. Redemptive community was diminished in favor of a social environment that looked upon any attempt to accept the reality of undulating spirituality as an instance of cheap grace. The only alternative that was left, whether it was named as such or not, was the dogged pursuit of the perfect, sanctified life. But since that is an unattainable reality, the church's only recourse is to pretend that it is succeeding in its management of sin – thus socializing its members to believe and behave as posers. Add to that the twin (revivalist) themes of *our despicable sinfulness* and *God's wrathful anger*, and you have the ingredients of shame-based spirituality that leaves little room for the belief that God loves us – *even likes us* – no matter how we fare in our attempts to live the sanctified life.

But this description of Christian spirituality is not without its detractors. "Hold on a minute," the critics will caution. "We can't take sin so lightly. This 'we're-only-amphibians-argument' is just a way of shirking responsibility for our lack of obedience to God's commands. Jesus said that we're supposed to be perfect as our Heavenly Father is perfect. When you say that we should make peace with our sinfulness and that God is actually okay with it, you're using grace as a license to sin."

It bears mentioning that the Apostle Paul's critics accused him of the same thing. But Paul's point in Romans 5 – 8 is that *knowing* what's right does not result in *doing* what's right. In fact Paul argues that the better we know God's law, the more inclined we are to disobey it. And the harder we try to live rightly before God, the more frustrated we become. Why? Because we cannot prevail over the flesh through fleshly means. Whenever we try to conquer our sinfulness through human effort, we empower the very thing we're trying to defeat. We invoke what Paul calls "the law of sin," which may be described as our fallen nature's inverse response to all godly effort.

We are intimately acquainted with this saboteur of the soul. We encounter it whenever we set out to lose a few pounds. Foods that we could pass over with hardly a glance become the object of our greatest desire as soon we tell ourselves we can't have them. We walk past a surface that bears the sign, "Wet Paint – Do Not Touch," and mysteriously we feel compelled to touch it. "I would not have known what coveting really was," says Paul, "if the law had not said, 'Do not covet.' But sin, seizing the opportunity afforded by the commandment, produced in my every kind of covetous desire" (Romans 7:7b, 8a).

Appealing to spiritual knowledge and human effort as the means of eradicating sin and living rightly before God has one benefit: it forces us to face our abject helplessness. Only then are we ready to throw ourselves on God's mercy. And when we do so, we acquire the one and only antidote to the law of sin – God's grace. This is Paul's point in Romans 8:

> Therefore, there is now no condemnation for those who are in Christ Jesus, because through Christ Jesus the law of the Spirit of life set you free from the law of sin and death. For what the law was powerless to do because it was weakened by the sinful nature, God did by sending his own Son in the likeness of sinful humanity to be a sin offering. And so he condemned sin in human flesh, in order that the righteous requirement of the law might be fully met in us, who do not live according to the sinful nature but according to the Spirit.
>
> Those who live according to the sinful nature have their minds set on what that nature desires; but those who live in accordance with the Spirit have their minds set on what the Spirit desires. (Romans 8:1–5)

We mustn't overlook the key point in the last verse of this citation. The phrase, "sinful nature" is literally "flesh." In Paul's thought, "flesh" is the law of sin's stomping ground, its sphere of influence. It will be that way until our "natural bodies" are raised in glory as "spiritual bodies" (see 1 Corinthians 15:42–44). For now we have to live with our flesh and the law of sin that drives it. But the gift of God's unmerited favor in Christ gives us a choice. We no longer have to worry about overcoming the flesh through fleshly effort. If we continue to "live according to the flesh" (i.e., if we keep trying to suppress our sinful urges through our own energy) we will continue to be consumed with "what the flesh desires." If, however, we "live according to the Spirit" (i.e., if we rest in the truth that God in Christ has already given us everything we need and will never deserve), we will find ourselves consumed with "the things of the Spirit." God's grace, in other words, packs a twofold punch: it *saves* us and it *sanctifies* us.

God isn't angry with us. He loves us. He proved it: "God demonstrates his own love for us in this: While we were still sinners, Christ died for us" (Romans 5:8). There's no need to pretend that we're something we're not. What we aren't is sinless; what we are is *loved*.

5. The Ouija Board

I have loved you with an everlasting love; I have drawn you with loving-kindness.

Jeremiah 31:3

When we allow ourselves to feel fully how we are being acted upon, we come in touch with a new life that we were not even aware was there.

Henri Nouwen, *Seeds of Hope*

Some Things make No Sense

God works in mysterious ways. We've heard this. Most of us, if we have been in Christ for any period of time, have experienced it. I've often wondered why the same One who had the power to raise Lazarus from the grave with the mere power of his spoken word had to make mud paste from his saliva to heal one blind man and to spit in the eyes of another and heal him in stages (compare John 11:43, 44; 9:1–7; and Mark 8:22–26). Why on one occasion did Jesus perform a miracle to prove to the unbelieving religious leaders that he had the authority to forgive sins and on another refuse to give them any miraculous sign at all (see Mark 2:1–12 and Matthew 12:38–40)? His interaction with demons is equally befuddling. At certain times Jesus forbids the demons to speak and on at least one occasion he carries on a conversation with them, negotiating an exit strategy (Mark 1:21–26, 32–34; and 5:1–13).

Over the years I've been equally curious as to why Jesus would have allowed my own interaction with the dark side to play such a vital role in my early spiritual formation. Mind you, faith for me did not begin as a reasoned decision. I grew up believing that God existed and that Jesus died and rose again for my salvation. But if I had harbored any doubts about the veracity of the biblical story, they were obliterated by an extraordinary experience that occurred when I was nineteen – an experience that paved the way for my receptiveness to the gospel roughly one year later.

Lessons from a Ouija Board

My friend, Manuel, and I were bored. We worked together at a local retail store. Manuel had been there since high school and helped me get a job shortly after we graduated. We had the day off and didn't have anything to do. Then I got the bright idea to go to the nearby shopping mall and buy a Ouija board. Years earlier my parents' friends had brought one to a party. I was fascinated by the prospect that it might actually serve as a gateway to the spiritual world. We brought it back to Manuel's house and set it up on his kitchen table. We sat across from each other and lightly placed our fingers on the triangular pointer device, called a planchette. Nothing happened. We read the directions to see if we had missed some key detail that would make the board operable. No missed cues. We tried again. Still nothing.

Manuel lived at home with his parents and two younger sisters, Ana and Maria. Before long his sisters arrived home from school. When Ana, the older of the two, came into the kitchen and saw what we doing, she exclaimed, "Oh is that a Ouija board? Let Maria play. It really works for her."

Manuel gave Maria his seat and I agreed to give it another go. Maria and I rested our fingertips on the planchette and immediately the game piece came to life. We asked the Ouija board all sorts of inane questions: What will the weather be like tomorrow? Guess what my favorite color is. Who was the president of the United States in 1812? The planchette seemed to move across the board all by itself. We were barely resting our fingers on it. In fact it felt at times that we were trying to keep up with it. Then I asked a yes-or-no question for which I wanted the answer "yes." The device started to move toward the word "no," so I pressed my fingers against it to direct it toward the desired answer. I was amazed at the force behind it. Whatever was driving the planchette had far more strength than Maria's little fingers could have produced. That's when I realized that something else – someone else – was moving the device.

The questions and answers gradually became more serious: How old will I be when I get married? What will her name be? In what year will I die? I was astonished when it knew the names of friends and family members that Maria could not have possibly known. Then I asked our invisible guest how he or she could know such things. "Who are you?" I prodded. The guest's answer was unnerving: "I am the devil."

Maria gasped and yanked her hands from the planchette as though it had become red hot. She didn't want to play any more. "Oh come on, Maria. Don't be so freaked out," I said. "What could happen? Here . . . put your fingers back on this thing for a second." Reluctantly she obliged. "Okay, let's get this straight," I probed, "you're really the devil?" Inexorably the planchette moved to the word yes. "Are you going to hurt us if we keep playing?" Just as steadily the piece moved to no. "See, Maria," I said reassuringly, "we don't have to worry about anything. Let's keep going, what do you say?" Maria agreed to keep playing for a few more minutes before taking leave to do homework.

I continued to query our would-be demon, "If you are the devil you obviously have great power, right?"

"Yes."

"In that case, can you prove it to us? Are you willing to give us a sign that demonstrates your power?"

"Yes."

Ana, who had been a silent observer up to this point, spoke out, "What are you doing, Chuck? You shouldn't be messing around with the devil. I don't want him to show us his power. Please stop this."

"Why are you guys such wimps?" I said, laughing. I spoke again to the third member of the game, "If you give us a sign of your power, will it scare us?"

"No."

"See? There's nothing to worry about," I said to Ana, who was seated, stiffly, to my left. Throughout the proceedings Manuel sat stone-faced to my right. He was sitting forward with his elbows on the table and his hands folded, covering his mouth. His dark brown eyes were fixed in a distant stare, watching intently for the slightest sign of paranormal activity. The tension in the room was thick.

I continued, "Will this be a sign we can see or will it be a sign we hear?"

The planchette lightened and started to move in counterclockwise circles, faster and faster, each revolution wider and faster than the one before it. Then with razor-sharp precision it landed on the letters in rapid succession: Y-O-U-W-I-L-L-S-E-E-I-T.

"Cool!" I said. "When will we see it?"

Again the game piece jumped to life in counterclockwise spins, landing with equal speed and precision: A-T-7.

We looked at the clock that was just to the left of the refrigerator above the kitchen sink. The time was 6:35 p.m. Where had the time gone? It felt like Maria and I had been playing no more than twenty minutes. We had actually been at it for two and a half hours. I also happened to take notice of the refrigerator. It was an off-yellow, jaundice color; adorned with about a dozen tiny fruit-shaped magnetic fasteners strewn randomly across the lower door. Hunger pangs prompted me to wonder what was inside. I wasn't the only one. We decided to take a break from the board and raid the refrigerator. Ana made us bologna and cheese sandwiches and we washed them down with orange soda. I helped Ana clean up and then we assumed our positions back at the table. This time Maria and I sat in opposite chairs – she in the chair I occupied earlier and I in hers. Manuel was now on my left and Ana was on my right. At 6:55 Maria and I readied ourselves and placed our fingers on the planchette. "Are you still there?" I asked.

No movement.

We waited another three minutes and asked again. Still nothing. At 7:00 sharp we gave it another try. The planchette moved directly to each letter in what seemed a less playful tone: T-U-R-N-O U T T H-E-L I G-H-1-S. The mood in the room instantly became more somber. Silently, Manuel looked at me to see if I wanted to continue. I reciprocated with an affirming nod. He reached back and flipped the switch on the wall. A single light in the living room sent a few, dim yellow rays in our direction, preventing the kitchen from going completely black. We were quite satisfied, however, that it was dark enough.

Maria and I sat with backs straight and fingers poised lightly on the planchette. After two or three very long minutes I asked, "Are you still there?"

"Yes."

"Are you still going to give us a sign of your power – a sign that we can see?"

"Yes."

"Will this sign scare us?" I was now asking as much for myself as I was for the others at the table.

"No."

The waiting dragged on. Every two or three minutes I asked our invisible guest if he was still present and if he still intended to show us a sign. Every time the answer was affirmative. We sat motionless around the table until 7:25. Finally, assuming that we had been duped, we gave up. Manuel reached over and turned on light.

At first none of us noticed it. Then Maria, whose seat faced the refrigerator, shrieked. Wide eyed, she pointed straight in front of her. We turned to see what she was looking at, and all at once we saw: the magnetic fruit fasteners, which had been scattered randomly over the refrigerator's lower door when we turned out the lights, were now positioned across the upper freezer door – forming the word "Ouija." I asked Maria to join me back at the Ouija board. We placed our fingers on the planchette and I asked, "Is this the sign?" Without hesitation the pointing device moved to its answer: "Yes." Then without bidding, it started to swirl in counterclockwise motions, landing on each letter with pointedly short hesitations: L-O-O-K-F-O-R-A-N-O-T-H-E-R-S-I-G-N-A-T-M-I-D-N-I-G-H-T.

I was back home and in bed when the clock struck midnight, but I wasn't sleeping. I lay there terrified. That is in fact the moment I first remembered the words of my high-school demonology teacher, Father Aquinas. A year earlier he had made the point that I alluded to earlier in this book: "The only way to overcome the forces of evil is through the one power in the universe that is greater – *God*." I prayed, "Jesus, please protect me from the devil. I don't want to see any more signs."

The Devil made me a Believer

Midnight came and went without incident – and from that point on I needed no convincing that the spiritual world existed. I knew it was real. It would be almost a year before my life would take any noticeable turn toward a relationship with God, but I consider the Ouija board experience at Manuel's house to be one of the truly significant events in my spiritual formation. It left me with no doubt that the portrayal of reality as it is presented in the biblical narrative is far more accurate than the distorted, spiritually neutered picture of reality embedded in the narrative of the modern Western world.

I must admit, however, that I have some misgivings about sharing my Ouija board experience. It borders on the insane. I realize that. I've shared this story with a few educated friends of mine here and there through my adult life. Most of them simply smile and say things like, "My! That's a . . . ah . . . well . . . that's a fantastic experience." Fantastic indeed! These friends don't actually think I made this up. Oh no. They think I lost my ID badge. I'm as sharp as a marble. I have bats in the belfry. I'm not hitting on all cylinders. I've lost the plot. I don't have both oars in the water. I'm one brick short of a load; one card shy of a full deck; one olive short of a pizza; one sandwich short of a picnic; one French fry short of a Happy Meal; one can short of a six pack; one wave short of a shipwreck. They're too nice to say it to my face, but when I suggest that the devil helped me become a believer, they think I'm as mad as a monkey on a tricycle. All they can do is politely invoke the universal expression of incredulity – "Wow."

Would Jesus really use the hater of my soul to liberate me from the clutches of the same? He can, of course. He's God. He can do anything. But would he? Here's where I've come down on this question: *Jesus uses whatever means he deems necessary to save one of his lambs from the enemy's snare.* Remember that it was Satan who induced Judas Iscariot to betray his friend, enacting the final stages of Jesus' atoning work. God has an established track record of turning evil on its head, using it for his ultimate good. Though the high priest Caiaphas had malice in his heart when he said, "it is better for one man to die for the people than that the whole nation perish," he was actually prophesying (see John 11:50–52). Jesus used the evil intentions of the rulers of his age to pull off the crucifixion. Had they known what God was up to, says the Apostle Paul, "they would not have crucified the Lord of glory" (1 Corinthians 2:8). Jesus used anything and everything to accomplish his saving purposes and express his tender mercies.

Jesus addresses every situation and every person the right way. He knows how best to respond to us in our respective life situations. No two people relate to Christ in exactly the same way. Nor does he relate to any two people in the same fashion. He is fully present to you as though you were the only one in his life. He hears your every heartbeat. Like he did with his friends, Mary and Martha, Jesus weeps when you weep. He feels every pang of sorrow and every joyful exultation. Even though he knows what you are going to pray long before you form the words, he is completely present to you in that moment, lovingly engaging your heart and soul as though nothing else in the universe existed.

A scene from Jim Carrey's 2003 blockbuster, *Bruce Almighty*, comes to mind. Newly deified Bruce is trying to figure out how to cope with all those voices in his head – the multitude of prayers, which are jamming his consciousness twenty-four hours a day. He tries organizing every prayer into files, only to find his living room crammed full of file cabinets with nary an inch to move. So he goes to Post-it notes, which swathe his entire house, including himself and his dog, in a sea of yellow sticky sheets. Then it occurs to him that routing the world's prayers through email is the way to go. At first check, he has over a million requests to process. He begins typing his responses with lightning fast precision – single-handedly at times. Convinced that he has made significant progress, he rechecks the count. To his dismay the count has soared to over three million. "What a bunch of whiners!" he exclaims. Then in desperation, he clicks "yes to all." The results are both humorous and horrifying.

In the movie's context, the point is that if God were to say "yes" to everybody's prayers the consequences would of course be disastrous. But this scene also raises the question of how exactly God is able to process all those prayers that bombard him day and night. I've heard Christians suggest that we shouldn't bother God with our trivial matters. "After all," they say, "God has more important things on his mind than your scrawny, little concerns." Such sentiments betray a very small view of God.

St. Paul says that we "live and move and have our being" in God (Acts 17:28). God is hardwired to every nook and cranny of his creation. Not a single sparrow falls to the ground without God's notice. He keeps tabs on the hair count of every human scalp. He's got a name for every star and for every electron in the universe. He tracks the blood pressure of every living creature that has a pulse. He is simultaneously tuned to every frequency. God hears every sound, feels every sensation, and senses very emotion. God smells every scent. God sees every sight. God knows every thought. God tastes every flavor. God is before all things, above all things, and in all things. Nothing exists apart from God. He is without beginning and without end, the Creator of all creation, the Truth of all truth, the Good of all that is good, the Holy of all that is holy, and the Power of all that is powerful. Moreover, God envelops all that does not exist and never will. He knows everything that will never happen – the infinity of possibilities that will never be. God is 100 percent present to everything at every moment. Nothing, absolutely nothing, transcends his existence or escapes his notice.

The opening statement of the last paragraph is telling. The words aren't Paul's own. He is actually quoting a famous Cretan poet, Epimenides, who lived and died some 600 years earlier. In doing so, Paul wasn't endorsing *everything* this poet ever said. Rather, he demonstrates a potent theological fact: God marshals everything at his disposal for his tender, saving purposes. God in the Fourth Gospel co-opted the concept of logos from pagan philosopher Heraclitus as a means of describing the most profound truth of all history – the Incarnation (see John 1:1–14). In Romans 12 he baptized the pagan principle *logikos*, using it to describe the Christian's practice of the presence of Christ (a theme we will return to later in this book). God used the greed and impatience of Judas Iscariot. God used the jealousy and ill will of a handful of religious leaders, the caprice of an ignorant mob, and the spinelessness of a Pontius Pilate to pull off the ultimate act of divine deception. And in my life, God used the devil to impel me into his saving embrace. There's nothing in your life that God cannot use to draw you into the safety of his all-powerful arms.

6. Belief on Steroids

Such confidence as this is ours through Christ before God. Not that we are competent in ourselves to claim anything for ourselves, but our competence comes from God. He has made us competent as ministers of a new covenant – not of the letter but of the Spirit; for the letter kills, but the Spirit gives life.

2 Corinthians 3:4–6

I acknowledge, Lord, and I give thanks that you have created your image in me, so that I may remember you, think of you, love you. But this image is so obliterated and worn away by wickedness, it is so obscured by the smoke of sins, that it cannot do what it was created to do, unless you renew and reform it. I am not attempting, O Lord, to penetrate your loftiness, for I cannot begin to match my understanding with it, but I desire in some measure to understand your truth, which my heart believes and loves.

Anselm of Canterbury, *Proslogion*

Candidate for Least-Likely-to-Succeed Award

Most seminary professors I know have more than a modest love of knowledge. That is certainly true of me. But it was not always so. If the people with whom I went to high school found out what I am doing these days, they would be forced to believe in God if they did not already. There can be no other way to account for the transformation from a pothead to an egghead. I have the distinction of graduating high school with the lowest allowable grade point average. One morning Father Landon, the teacher of our senior drama course, kicked me out of his class in a screaming rage after my friend, Tom Smith, and I tried to ad-lib a short play with only the names of the characters memorized. We had invented scripts on the fly many times before and were doing a reasonably convincing job of it that day. There is no doubt we would have pulled it off that time too had it not been for one small detail: Father Landon had obtained his own copy of the script.

Father Landon was a gruff old priest with a raspy voice and a rotund figure. He loved his cigars and – by the looks of his varicose face – he loved his potent potables as well. You could always gauge Landon's disposition by the color of his face and balding pate. His head was essentially a mood ring – and red was not his happy color. I had never seen Father Landon so upset. "Where's your script? Where's your script?" he barked, his face and head radiated a crimson glow that was actually starting to turn purple.

Tom tried to explain, though I have no idea what he possibly could have said in that moment to placate Father Landon's wrath. "Let me explain . . ." was all Tom could get out of his mouth before Father Landon rose from his seat at the back of the classroom and headed toward us. He growled and clenched his jaw so tightly that it made his teeth show and his jowls protrude and quiver. Father Landon had turned into a pit bull, and we were the canine cleric's prey. "Get out! Get out! Get out!" he screeched. Clutching the script of our play in his right fist, he waved it, pugilistically, as though he wished it were a club. His howling voice was shrill and broken; pushed beyond its limit. Tom and I took a final bow and the class erupted in a standing ovation. We made it out the door with Father Landon nipping at our heels. He stopped at the classroom door and shouted at us as we ran down the breezeway, "You two are *finished*. Do you hear me? *Finished*! I never, ever want to see you back in class."

Later that day I met with my guidance counselor, Sister JoAnn, to inform her that Father Landon had expelled me from his class. "That's very bad news, Chuck," she said shaking her head. "You need that class to graduate. You better find out how to get back into Father Landon's good graces or you can forget about graduating this June." I told her that I didn't care whether I finished high school. I said as much to my mother that night. She, however, was not about let her oldest child and only son go into the world without a high school diploma. So she single-handedly worked through the class textbook and typed out reports on every chapter. The finished piece was at least twenty-five pages long. My mother gave me strict orders to deliver the document to the school secretary who would in turn make sure that it got to Father Landon.

Several days later I sheepishly approached my estranged instructor. He spoke softly – his face and head remained a healthy flesh tone. "I got your chapter reviews. Very impressive. I don't want you back in class but I'll give you a passing grade. Good luck."

I met Sister JoAnn in the counseling office hallway a few months later, just before the school's commencement. "Bet you never thought I'd make it through high school," I chided in good nature. Straight-faced, she answered with uncanny sincerity, "Honestly, Chuck, I didn't think you would ever graduate." She wasn't alone. If my high school had conferred the least-likely-to-succeed-in-life award, the prize would have probably gone to me.

Belief takes Center Stage

The beginning of my faith journey at age twenty marks both a spiritual and intellectual awakening. Although in the past I had started to read several books, I never finished a single one. But when I started reading the Bible that Merriam gave me, I could not put it down. My poor reading skills actually worked to my advantage. I had to read the Bible slowly – it was the only way I could read. Yet that slow, ruminating pace enabled me to absorb and remember almost everything I read. It took almost a year to get through the Bible the first time, but even now, more than thirty years later, I have no shame in saying that the Bible is the first book that I *finished*. I didn't comprehend the implications at first, but I later came to realize that finishing the Bible that first time set the stage for everything else to come.

My intellectual curiosity as a young adult was not based on the quest to prove to myself or to others that it was reasonable to believe what I believed. My upbringing as a Roman Catholic – and the Ouija board experience at Manuel's house – established the legitimacy of my beliefs beyond any reasonable doubt. My quest to learn is best summed up in Anselm's motto, "faith seeking understanding," which was as much his prayer as it was an intellectual enterprise:

> I am not attempting, O Lord, to penetrate your loftiness, for I cannot begin to match my understanding with it, but I desire in some measure to understand your truth, which my heart believes and loves. For I do not seek to understand in order that I may believe, but I believe in order to understand. For this too I believe, that unless I believe, I shall not understand.[1]

To quote St. Anselm is to make my theological journey out to be much holier and purer than it has actually turned out to be. The most basic point is that my pursuit of knowledge has arisen out of the conviction that faith is primary and the pursuit to understand that faith more deeply is secondary. To be sure, I have had to make some big adjustments to what I believe along the way, but the core (as I have judged it at least) remains intact. I have also learned that it is inadequate to conceive of theology as merely the process of justifying our beliefs *as the means of ensuring that we believe the right things.* I consider this the modern church's wrong turn toward the idolatry of belief, which may be defined as the elevation of human belief to divine status. Of course, no sensible Christian would admit that they have so elevated the place of belief, but our *practiced* theology is more revealing than our *professed* theology.

Curious George – an Anabaptist of a Different Sort

A case in point is the encounter I had with a well-meaning teacher of an adult Bible class. Manuel and I had made our about-face for Christ at roughly the same time a year earlier. But since we lived so far from each other we each decided to find a church that was closer to our own homes. After my departure from Catholicism I landed at a local Baptist Church. I respected the pastor's knowledge of Scripture and had started building some friendships. In spring of that year I was baptized along with a half-dozen other disciples. Manuel was a bit slower in finding a church close to home, but he finally started to attend a church whose commitment to following the Bible seemed extraordinary. Manuel called one Wednesday afternoon to invite me to the church's adult Bible study that night. I happily accepted and followed his directions to the building.

I arrived about ten minutes early. The structure's exterior was strikingly unpretentious – a two-story, tan-colored stucco building. The sanctuary was on the top floor and the classrooms were below. Eight or ten refurbished school buses bearing the church's insignia were parked side by side in the lot just to the north. There was no stained glass, no cross – nothing that distinguished it as a Christian church other than the group's descriptor, which was painted in black letters on the front of the building: "The Church of Christ Meets Here." Within a few minutes Manuel arrived, taking the parking place alongside mine. We entered together. The first interior feature I noticed was the carpet. It was worn and threadbare; a light, pea-soup-green color. The inside of the building was equally devoid of telltale imagery – no pictures of Jesus, no cross, no candles – it was even more spartan than the Baptist Church I was attending. It was in fact the exact Christian opposite of the Roman Catholic Church.

We made our way to the classroom downstairs and were greeted warmly by everyone in the room. The teaching and conversation was lively. I felt the freedom to participate and the group seemed to appreciate my input. I had just completed my first reading of the Bible and was excited to share my newfound knowledge with others. I also believed myself to be a reliable judge of orthodoxy on behalf of my good friend who was considering whether to make this group his permanent church home.

After the class was over we gathered in the upstairs sanctuary with all the others, young and old, who had met in separate classes. The singing was like nothing I had ever experienced. It was completely a cappella. The entire group sang – instinctively it seemed – in four-part harmony. I thought to myself, "It's a good thing these people know how to sing. Apparently they can't afford a piano or organ." After the singing was over the pastor gave a short message and closed with prayer. I was impressed. This group obviously put more stock in their relationships with each other and their outreach to the community – as evidenced in a thriving bus ministry that drew hundreds of children from the surrounding neighborhoods – than on brick-and-mortar frills that drain the coffers of so many other churches.

But appearances and impressions aside, I wanted to make sure – for Manuel's sake – that these folks were on the theological up and up. Most people lingered after the evening's festivities had ended. I struck up a conversation with George, the teacher of the adult Bible class. He looked like an engineer. He had thick black-rim glasses. His white, short-sleeve button-down shirt was wrinkled from a long day at work. The left pocket sagged under the weight of a plastic penholder that carried several distinct writing instruments. He was medium build, perhaps a bit overweight, with thinning hair and a thick black beard. I asked him what his church thought about the Bible. Do they consider it inspired? Do they follow any other book besides the Bible? I asked him about their understanding of God. Do they believe in the Trinity?

George answered each question carefully and caringly. He assured me that his church considered the Bible to be the only inspired authority. He quoted their motto: "We speak where the Bible speaks, and we're silent where the Bible is silent." I said I liked that saying – it had a nice ring to it. He went on to say that they typically don't use the word Trinity because it is not in the Bible. They prefer the word "Godhead," because it speaks to the idea of God's (triune) nature and is found in Scripture (at least in the King James rendering of Colossians 2:9). I was surprised that they chose not to use the language of post New Testament councils, but was satisfied that the church met the benchmark of orthodoxy. It would be a good place for my friend, Manuel. We bid George a good night and headed for our cars. What happened next came as a surprise to say the least.

We were halfway back to our cars when George called my name. I turned around and saw him standing with his right arm lifted and his index finger sticking up, as though he were pointing to something in the night sky or giving me the number one signal. I looked up in the direction he seemed to be pointing and saw nothing. "That's odd," I thought to myself. I replied by smiling and giving him the thumbs-up sign. He shook his head to indicate that I had missed his point. Then, still holding up his arm, he spoke, "Chuck, I question your baptism." Manuel and I looked at each other in wonderment. I shrugged my shoulders and walked back to George. Manuel followed.

I asked George why he would be troubled about my baptism. Was he disturbed by my baptism as an infant in the Roman Catholic Church or by my recent baptism in the Baptist Church? He said he was concerned mostly with the latter. When I asked him why, he countered with a question, "Were you saved before or after you were baptized?" It was an easy answer I thought. "I was saved *before* I was baptized, of course." George frowned and answered, "Well that's the problem. The Bible teaches that baptism is the point at which a person is saved." He went on to cite several passages in the New Testament that appeared to support his point.

I remembered reading these passages and frankly had not known what to make of them. I had no idea why the Apostle Peter would have said to the first would-be followers of Jesus Christ, "Repent and be baptized, every one of you, in the name of Jesus Christ for the forgiveness of your sins" (Acts 2:38). Was Peter saying that baptism in water *forgives sin*? I was equally baffled when Peter likened baptism to the renewing effects of Noah's flood, in which "only a few people, eight in all [Noah and his family], were saved through water, and this water symbolizes baptism that now saves you also . . ." (1 Peter 3:20, 21). *Baptism saves us*? And I simply did not know how to interpret Ananias's invitation to Saul (who would later be named the Apostle Paul): "And now what are you waiting for? Get up, be baptized and wash your sins away, calling on his name" (Acts 22:16). *Baptism washes away sin*? What George said made sense. Unlike the others that I had consulted about these problem passages, George and his church simply accepted them at face value.

I checked my watch and noticed that it was almost 9:00 p.m. Feeling the need to bring the conversation to a close, I thanked George for shedding light on these important passages and assured him that I would have much more appreciation for my recent baptism in the Baptist Church.

"Hold on!" George snapped, "That baptism doesn't count for anything. That's why I said I question your baptism."

I asked him why he thought my baptism would not count. It was performed by immersion in water – the same mode required by George and his church. It was done as an act of obedience, as George described. What was missing? George went on to explain that people are immersed in water all the time – when they swim in a lake or fall into a dunk tank at the carnival. "Events like that don't count as baptism," George explained, "because these people don't believe that their sins are being washed away."

"Of course not," I answered, "but these aren't sacred events. When I got baptized it was very special. I did it in obedience to Jesus Christ and as a way of publicly declaring my faith in him. Are you saying that if I did not know at the time I was baptized that baptism saves me, it doesn't count – *you're saying I just got wet*?"

Sensing that I would not be pleased with his answer, George pursed his lips, raised his eyebrows, and gave an affirming nod. He continued, "We can't turn back the clock, Chuck. People get wet for all sorts of reasons. Sometimes it's to cool off. At other times it's to bathe. Some people swim for exercise. And when you were baptized, you did not get in the water to be saved. You got in the water for something else. You had all the best of intentions, I'm sure, but the bottom line is that you didn't get in the water for the right reason."

I began to wonder if it were not for some greater, providential purpose that I had visited the church that night.

Had God led me there to discover an essential truth that I had missed? I could find no good reason to resist this new teaching. It was, after all, the most straightforward way to interpret these passages. And though I was troubled by the implications of George's logic, I had no satisfactory rebuttal.

It was past 9:30 p.m. and work was coming early the next day. So I asked George when their next baptism service was scheduled. His eyes brightened and he said that the church did not have scheduled baptisms because, like Philip and the Ethiopian eunuch, he pointed out, "we baptize people whenever they are ready to be saved. The baptistery is ready to go. We can baptize you right now."

"Really? You've got to be kidding," I said. "It's almost 10 o'clock."

George smiled, "Paul baptized the Philippian jailor and his family in the middle of the night. Let me make some calls. I'm sure there are a few others who would want to be here for this."

Manuel had been quietly listening to the conversation. I asked him what he thought. He said he wanted to be baptized. I did too. George made the calls and within minutes several joyful faces had gathered in the sanctuary to witness our baptisms.

Trusting versus Thinking

The decision to be baptized that night forever changed the course of my life. In retrospect I am convinced that I was rightly related to Jesus Christ well before either of my baptism-by-immersion experiences. But I am forever indebted to that tradition – known as "the churches of Christ" – for the many profound contributions it made to my life and faith. Some of the finest Christians I know belong to this movement, which continues to thrive in its work of making disciples. The churches of Christ received me from the arms of Roman Catholicism and provided formational nurture that benefits me as a Christian to this day. I have also discovered that the very theological issues that drove me from that fellowship in

1990 are alive and well, to greater or lesser degrees, in the larger Christian world.

George's logic is symptomatic of a belief system that has infiltrated the church, Catholic and Protestant, with the fatally flawed notion that "we have to get it right in terms of what we believe or else." "Belief" in this instance is equivalent to "intellectual assent." If we do not *think the right way* about a given article of faith or doctrine, we're out of luck. This logic gives credit to whom credit is not due – namely, *to us.* For nearly 500 years the church in the West has been stymied by the same intellectual agendas that have set the marching orders for the wider culture. And in almost every case, the guiding ideal has been the quest for certainty. While these agendas have had a variety of effects on the church, George's description of baptism perfectly exemplifies one such effect: *The rite isn't right if our thinking isn't right.* According to George's theology, my first immersion experience did not count because I was not thinking all the right things at the moment the pastor plunged me into the baptismal waters. Belief, in other words, must be *complete* to be of any redeeming value.

What I am about to say next will make some Christians very nervous – and justifiably so. They worry that I might be building a case for the proposal that what we believe doesn't really matter. Or worse yet, they will (wrongly) hear me claiming that there's no such thing as absolute truth. Issues of faith and truth are of ultimate concern to us. So let me offer the following assurances.

I believe that truth in Christ is absolute. Jesus said, "I am the way and the truth and the life. No one comes to the Father except through me" (John 14:6). That is true whether one accepts it or not. Scripture unequivocally stipulates that what we believe has eternal implications: "Whoever believes in him is not condemned, but whoever does not believe stands condemned already because they have not believed in the name of God's one and only Son" (John 3:18). Moreover, because of Jesus Christ I am not the same person that took his final bow in Father Landon's high-school drama class. I have dedicated my adult life to the pursuit of knowledge and to the faithful handling of the word of truth (see 2 Timothy 2:15).

With that said, we must weigh contemporary notions of Christian belief against the biblical witness. Belief as it is conceived in Scripture has quite a bit more to do with *trust* than *thought*. Like most of our words in the English language, the New Testament word for "belief," and its verbal counterpart, "believe," encompass a wide range of meaning. The same noun and verb are translated "faith" and "to have faith." Sometimes the word conveys the idea of faithfulness (noun) or being faithful (verb). Less often it speaks to the idea of giving credence to something or someone or to thinking that something is true. In rare instances (such as Acts 17:31), the word even means "proof" or "evidence." But most often, especially when the New Testament speaks of believing in Jesus Christ, the primary nuance of the word is *trust*. If we were to map the nuances of the biblical word for belief in the form of an expanding set of concentric circles – the primary nuance being at the center and less frequent meanings occupying the outer rings in descending order – we would get something like this:

Belief as it is often conceived of today, however, consists of giving intellectual assent to doctrinal statements that are considered theologically correct. Our *certainty* as Christians rests, in other words, on our confidence that we have the right beliefs. We condemn certain "sects" for believing incorrect things about Jesus and surmise that these erroneous convictions will likely keep those who hold them from going to heaven. Perhaps that is true, but I would wish no one to be condemned for holding errant or incomplete beliefs about Jesus Christ. I am certainly not prepared to say that everything I believe is correct. One friend puts his finger on the conundrum we face when he says, "I know that my theology is at least 80 percent correct; I just don't know where the other 20 percent is hiding." Questions of orthodoxy have their place, to be sure, but contemporary understandings of belief have set a standard too high for any of us to achieve. In contrast to Scripture's conception of belief, our view, influenced as it is by Western philosophy, appears to be the exact opposite, as illustrated below:

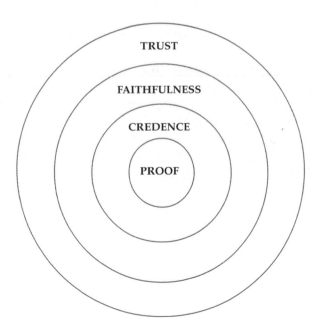

TRUST

FAITHFULNESS

CREDENCE

PROOF

Debates about the nature of truth and "how we know what we know" are philosophical ones. I find it ironic that those who claim to be vanguards of "postmodernism" (or whatever else we may call it) have chosen a modern philosophical route to justify their new proposals. They, no less than their "modern" counterparts, appeal to methods that help us think ourselves straight. After years of study and reflection on these matters I have found myself coming full circle. Or better yet, I have circled the mountain one full time in my upward ascent toward understanding and have found that the higher altitude this time around affords a better view. Or perhaps I'm just suffering from altitude sickness. In any event, I am finding the proposition of an ever-widening cultural, philosophical, and ideological gap between so-called modern and postmodern worlds to be more and more difficult to accept. I am prepared to say, cautiously, that all such talk is unhelpful for two reasons: *it fractures community* – especially Christian community and *it is not true*. Almost everything that assumes the epithet "postmodern" (besides art and architecture) seems to be more most-modern than postmodern.

I say more about my altitude-induced perspective in the following chapters. The point here is that appeals to Western philosophy have distorted the biblical image of belief, prompting people to conceive of it more in terms of *thinking* than of *trusting*. It is a matter of emphasis, and when the emphasis is out of kilter, the focus is off target – in this case with devastating consequences. As Leonard Sweet has said on many occasions, when God gave us the truth in its ultimate form, he did so by sending a person, not a proposition. When thinking our way clear on propositional truth takes priority over celebrating our relationship with the Person of truth, our "belief" may be edging into idolatry.

7. The "Most-Modern" Age

*What has been will be again, what has been done will be done again;
there is nothing new under the sun. Is there anything of which one
can say, "Look! This is something new?" It was here already, long
ago; it was here before our time.*

Ecclesiastes 1:9, 10

*History is more or less bunk. It's tradition. We don't want tradition.
We want to live in the present and the only history that is worth a
tinker's damn is the history we made today.*

Henry Ford, Interview in the *Chicago Tribune*, May 25, 1916

Postmodern Pilgrimage

The discovery of some new insight, one that few others have
access to, can be a heady experience. It can leave us feeling
good about ourselves and somewhat impatient toward those
who for whatever reason haven't yet gotten it. I have been
on the receiving end of such impatience on more than one
occasion. But as I reflect on the point I made in the last
chapter – namely, that it is unhelpful to conceive of an ever-
widening gap between the "modern" and "postmodern"
because it fractures community and because it is not true
– one particular experience comes to mind.

I had just begun my PhD studies at Fuller Theological
Seminary, in Pasadena, California. At a luncheon a few
months earlier Richard Hughes, Distinguished Professor of
Religion at Pepperdine University, mentioned that James
Wm. McClendon, Jr. had recently joined the faculty at Fuller.
Richard asked me if I was familiar with McClendon's work.

I was not. He asked if I had already secured a faculty mentor. I told him that Ray Anderson, Professor of Practical Theology at Fuller, had already agreed to serve in that role. Then Richard said, "Chuck, you want to find out if there is any way to work with McClendon. There is no one in the world more qualified to advise you on the topic you want to pursue."

Richard and I had not known each other that long, but I respected his opinion. I looked up to him as a great scholar and a caring confidant who had taken time from his busy schedule to help me process some difficult decisions. I trusted that he would steer me in the right direction in this instance.

The first opportunity to meet Professor McClendon was at the new-student orientation for incoming doctoral students. I approached him after the meeting and said that Richard Hughes had recommended that I get to know him. Dr. McClendon smiled and said, "If Richard Hughes said we should meet, we should meet." At the orientation meeting each student was called upon to present his or her proposed research topic to the large, intimidating panel of professors. Dr. McClendon, I noticed, had paid particular attention to my presentation.

Jim, as he would later insist that I call him, was a tall southern gentleman with silver-white hair and a neatly groomed beard and mustache. He spoke with a deep, smooth voice. A faint drawl betrayed his Louisiana roots. He was sixty-six at the time we first met. I repeated what Richard said – that he was the best person to advise me on my chosen topic. I asked if he would consider working with me in some capacity, possibly as my secondary mentor. He said he would think about it and get back to me.

A few days later Jim called to set up an appointment. When we met he said that he had given my proposal a lot of thought and would be willing to work with me under one condition – that he be my primary advisor. I found myself in an awkward position. I could continue with my present mentor, Ray Anderson, and miss out on what my friend Richard said was the opportunity of a lifetime, or I could fracture my relationship with the one person who had opened the way for me to be at Fuller in the first place. I felt stuck. Finally I mustered the courage to have a candid conversation with Ray.

No sooner had I described the situation than Ray came to my rescue. He said he would gladly work with me in whatever capacity was best. "Now that Professor McClendon is here," he said, "I am happy to serve as your secondary mentor. Don't worry about that a bit." I was relieved – and happy to be working with both Jim and Ray. It was the best of all possible scenarios. And in the seven years it took to complete my degree, I profited immensely from Ray's input. To this day I am grateful for his generous spirit in that matter.

Jim had just started writing the second volume of what would be his three-volume magnum opus. He asked me to join the group that reviewed portions of the manuscript as he produced it. He assured me that this would be as important a part of the mentoring process as any other aspect of the doctoral program. I gladly accepted. Jim modeled a way of engaging in reflection and writing that few scholars seemed to be using. He wrote his books in dialog with peers and students. Every four weeks or so, each member of the group would receive a thick envelope in the mail containing the latest portion of Jim's work. We were expected to read it carefully and be prepared to offer constructive input when we met in his home for what he called "reflection and a simple meal."

The meals were anything but simple. The discussions lasted about ninety minutes. Around the forty-five-minute mark Jim's wife, Nancey, would start working her magic in the kitchen. Before long, aromas of the most delectable cuisines wafted into the living room where we were seated, making the last portion of scholarly conversation agonizingly slow. After the session was over Jim invited us into the breakfast nook adjacent to the kitchen for wine and cocktails. The group engaged in rather stiff small talk. When the food was ready we moved to the dining room. The table was adorned with a white embroidered tablecloth, antique china, crystal wine and water glasses, and fine silverware. Various eating utensils were placed on the table in different spots and at different angles, signaling their proper use. At each course the appropriate wine for that segment of the meal was served. Those of us who joined Jim and Nancey for this simple meal had to bat through the mental cobwebs to retrieve what little we remembered of Emily Post's advice on etiquette and manners – all the while maintaining a calm exterior.

The meetings at Jim and Nancey's home turned out to be more formative than any other educational experience in the doctoral program. But the first few sessions were, in a word, painful. When I applied to the doctoral program at Fuller, I was confident that I would succeed. I had graduated seminary at the top of my class and had, I believed, a reasonably comprehensive grasp of the Christian theological enterprise. The meetings at Jim's house turned my world sideways, humbling – even humiliating – me. It seemed that I was the only member of the group that consistently didn't get it. I was repeatedly mystified as to why a given course of conversation was pursued. The group raised issues that made no sense and left other matters, which I considered central to the subject, untouched. Whenever I weighed in with a comment, they would pause and acknowledge my remark with a polite, expressionless stare, and then pick up where they left off. It was as though they were speaking another language, and everyone understood it except me.

The group's apparent lack of interest in my ideas prompted me to reciprocate by formulating my own unspoken criticisms. I studied each person around the room, one by one, and was troubled by what I saw. "Was I like them?" I wondered. It didn't take a rocket scientist to see that each one was extraordinarily brilliant and well read. But it was equally apparent (at least it seemed so at the time) that this was a group of social misfits. I returned home after the third meeting and declared to my wife, Dianne, "I don't want to become an egghead." Before the meeting that day Jim had met with me privately to suggest that I do more listening than talking. It was obvious that everyone in the group was privy to insights that simply refused to yield their mysteries to me.

Then all at once there was a gestalt – an epiphany if you will – in which all things became new. Jim was experiencing a bit of a dry spell with his writing in the fourth month of our meetings and had nothing for the group to review at the scheduled time. But instead of canceling the get-together, Jim suggested that we read and discuss a chapter from Stanley Fish's famous book, *Is There a Text in this Class?*[1] Fish is a literary theorist who gained notoriety for his proposal that "interpretive communities" play a huge role in the formation of "interpretive strategies." All I can say is that Fish's work became the interpretive key that opened the lock to everything that we had been discussing over the past few months. At once everything made sense. The group soon recognized that I was able to track with their discussions and offer input that helped to move the conversation forward. I had now effectively caught what I could not be taught. The mystics of postmodernism had finally admitted me to their elite guild.

Drawing Lines in the Sands of Time

It wasn't long before I started to observe how many people were still in the dark with regard to postmodernism. On one occasion, Jim attended a student's ordination council. One of the senior members of my denomination's leadership was interviewing the young man. "We've heard you say a lot about God's immanence," the official queried the ordinand, "but what about his transcendence?" Jim recounted to me afterwards that the man's question sounded as though it had come straight from the nineteenth century. We had a good laugh. I felt privileged to be in the know.

The more I learned the easier it became for me to distinguish between the modern and the postmodern. While I felt a growing affinity toward those who shared my newfound knowledge, I was becoming increasingly impatient with those who didn't get it. I could even sniff out the phonies who claimed to be postmodern but weren't by a long shot. Soon it became a small step to move from distinguishing the modern from the postmodern to distancing myself in heart and spirit from the likes of every unenlightened modernist. Although I could not avoid these people entirely, my interaction with them was checked by an us–them cynicism. With the aid of other like-minded postmodernists, I drew the modern–postmodern line between the professors at Fuller Seminary, fellow pastors, members of my church's leadership team, and between the members of the church I pastored.

At the same time I noticed that some modernists had begun to cast a suspicious eye toward the ever-growing number of Christian postmodernists. They started to accuse postmodern Christians of abandoning the belief in transcendent truth. I found this accusation absurd, since I for one had certainly not surrendered the conviction that truth in its ultimate form (as it exists in God) is transcendent. The question for me was not whether transcendent truth exists, but rather how well human beings are able to comprehend that truth. My conversion to postmodernism had left me with the realization that there is no such thing as pure objectivity. We do not – we *cannot* – look at the world through clear lenses.

Our perception of reality is not only limited by our five senses, it is also confined by the factors particular to who we are as embodied selves – by our time and place in history, by our families of origin and the friends and communities that influenced us in our formative years, by our innate intelligence, by our gender, by our ethnicity. The list goes on. In every instance, we come to terms with who we are and what we believe amid a variety of intersecting social contexts that meet us at the point of our embodiedness. While truth in its ultimate form may be infinite and transcendent, our *grasp* of it is, in a word, finite.

But so far as the modernist Christians were concerned, postmodern Christians weren't merely saying that truth is socially *comprehended*; they claimed that postmodern Christians were saying that truth is socially *constructed* – which is to say that there's no such thing as "Truth" (with a capital T) at all.

While I could not speak for all postmodern Christians at the time, I knew that this accusation was false so far as I and the postmodernists I hung around with were concerned.

Lines in the Sand become Battle Lines

In the years since my postmodern epiphany I have seen the tensions between modern Christians and postmodern Christians only intensify. Not long ago one of my colleagues at George Fox University invited me to a meeting with his pastor and several other church leaders in the area. It was an informal gathering, a barbecue, at the pastor's house. Several guests were already there when we arrived. The house was nestled in a thickly wooded neighborhood in one of the more exclusive sections of the Portland metro area. High ceilings, abundant windows, and rustic interior wood trim gave the home the look and feel of a mountain lodge. The large, tiled island in the kitchen was laden with all sorts of scrumptious foods that reflected the pastor's taste for quality as much as quantity. His college-age son greeted us at the door and led us into the kitchen. He was bright, articulate, and confident. I could tell that he was very much at home in the company of older Christian adults – a quality that I have always admired in my own children, Krystal, Matthew, and Nathan.

As we stood in area between the kitchen and family room, my colleague introduced me to the others. Within minutes the rest of the guests arrived. Handshakes, hugs, and lots of laughter made it apparent that these people enjoyed being with each other. Soon the pastor emerged from the deck outside the family room with a platter of steaming chicken, fresh off the barbecue. Oohs and ahhs signaled a marked spike in the room's hunger pangs. My colleague adeptly waited for the pastor to transfer the large plate to his wife before making introductions. The pastor greeted me heartily with a smile and firm handshake. He exuded a sweet balance of friendliness and confidence. I saw right away that this man was the model from whom his son acquired his social skills.

The pastor gave thanks for the food and we filled our plates and headed into the dining room. The table was large enough to accommodate the entire group. Conversation over the meal remained lighthearted and friendly. I learned a little bit about each person – where they were from, which churches they pastored, and what they enjoyed doing for fun. The pastor's son also joined us at the table and actively participated in the conversation. During dessert I learned of the pastor's taste for fine coffee and enjoyed savoring one of his favorite blends. After the meal we cleared the table of everything but our coffee cups and the conversation shifted to the designated subject – a review of *Church in the Emerging Culture: Five Perspectives*. The book is edited by Leonard Sweet and features the views of several influential contemporary thinkers.[2] Several members of the group displayed the copious notes they had taken on the book.

I sensed a change of mood around the table – from jovial to serious. It soon became apparent that none in the room, except my colleague and me, were favorably disposed toward things "emergent" or postmodern. They took particular exception to Brian McLaren, who in their estimation is the infamous ringleader of the ragtag band of emergent disciples. And because I was introduced to the group as a friend of Leonard Sweet and the director of a doctoral program in "Leadership in the Emerging Culture," I began to feel the weight of their stares. It was like I had a bull's-eye painted on my chest and the modern warriors were readying their arrows for the kill. My colleague had invited me to "a postmodern barbecue," as he put it. But only in that moment did I realize that I might in fact be the one on the grill. I felt conspicuously out of place.

The pastor raised strong objections to McLaren's notion of truth, suggesting that he was leading countless young people astray with teachings that bordered on heresy. Then he leaned forward and asked me pointedly, "Chuck, what do you think about McLaren's teaching?" My initial answer, I'm sure, did not help my cause. "Well . . .," I said, stalling, "I think you guys might be misunderstanding Brian. He's basically trying to account for truth in the light of non-foundationalist epistemology." No sooner had the words left my mouth than I realized how out of place they were. The pastor betrayed his incredulity by raising his eyebrows and squeezing both eyes shut for a second. Then he opened his eyes and said with a smirk, "Would you mind putting that in simpler terms for us uneducated folks?" The pastor was by no means unsophisticated. Neither was anyone else at the table.

I gathered myself and came at it again, "I'm sorry. What I mean is that Brian is not denying the existence of transcendent truth. He believes the same thing we do about truth. He's trying to help us recognize that no human being has the ability to comprehend truth in its totality. We are finite beings trying to understand infinite truth. As Paul says, 'we see in a glass darkly.'" I could tell that some at the table were ready to accept my explanation, but the pastor continued to press the issue. He insisted that Brian had written certain things that could only be interpreted as a rejection of absolute truth. The others nodded in agreement. Overall these men were delightfully hospitable and good natured, but there was no convincing them that Brian – and other likeminded postmodernists – was not profoundly off base in his interpretation of the nature of truth. I did not express how I felt to the group that night, but I was quite frustrated by the whole affair. My colleague, on the other hand, got an earful on the drive home.

The experience that night stirred some misgivings that had been brewing for quite some time about the whole modern–postmodern divide. Here was a pastor who was leading a church that effectively engaged what is by all accounts an emergent (postmodern) crowd. The pastor's son certainly qualifies as a member of that demographic by every conceivable measure. I learned from my colleague on the drive home that the church's worship services meet the emerging-church criteria in terms of being "experiential, participatory, image-driven, and connective."[3] And they are committed to robust "go-and-be" initiatives that empower the members to rub elbows with a multitude of non-Christians who would likely profess to be spiritual but not religious.

My colleague and I settled back into our own thoughts for the remainder of the drive home. For my part, I began to develop a list of churches that fell into the same general category as my colleague's church – churches that are *culturally* emergent but *convictionally* modern. Then it dawned on me: the chief dividing line between the modern and postmodern church is arbitrary. The reason why so many modern-church and emergent-church people talk past each other is because they have committed themselves to two different ways of construing human knowledge – *and both ways are equally modern*.

The philosophical name for what I am describing here is "epistemology," a term that was first coined in 1856 by philosopher James F. Ferrier. It is derived from two Greek words, *episteme* (knowledge) and *logos* (an ordered account or explanation). Epistemology is the branch of philosophy that is concerned with knowledge – "how do we know what we know?" From the seventeenth century through the better part of the twentieth century, one particular way of construing knowledge was predominant. The primary assumption of this approach is that certain facts are "basic" – that is, they are like the foundation or bedrock of everything else we know. Another important assumption of this method is that these foundational facts can be accessed by anybody who rightly uses the tools of reason. Those who accept this philosophy of knowledge believe that it holds the key to objective truth, which we can embrace with unwavering certainty.

Christians made good use of this approach to knowledge for almost 400 years. In the seventeenth century, it provided a way for disciples gain some certainty about what they believed amid a world social and political upheaval. In the eighteenth century it helped to establish the legitimacy of Christian theology as a valid branch of learning alongside other disciplines in the newly formed research universities. In the nineteenth and twentieth centuries, it was the backbone of almost all academic and popular Christian teaching. A detailed explanation of this approach, called "foundationalism," can be extremely complex and confusing – even to philosophers. But the point is that we have benefited profoundly from this approach.

Of course it is only fair to ask, then, why this method is now being called into question, if in fact it was so helpful to Christians for the past 400 years. The reason is because throughout the second half of the twentieth century thinkers in a variety of disciplines began to question whether "basic beliefs" even existed. The more they probed the matter, the more they were convinced that the only thing "basic" to our knowledge as human beings is the social, cultural, and linguistic structures that serve as our mind's operating system. So far as these thinkers are concerned, we do not know what we know by thinking our way clear on basic beliefs and then engaging in various exercises of rationality from there. We learn to communicate, to think, to value, and to believe the way we do from our immediate and extended social environments. These thinkers concluded that there is simply no such thing as basic beliefs that are universally available through the tools of reason.[4] What struck me that night in my colleague's car – as if for the first time – was something I that had learned years earlier in my study of philosophy. This so-called new-and-improved approach to knowledge is every bit as "modern" as the "basic beliefs" approach – in fact it pre-dates it by over a hundred years.

I am indebted to British mathematician and philosopher Stephen Toulmin for this insight. He takes issue with the standard historical account of the modern age and its beginning, calling many of its assumptions exaggerated or even downright false. He convincingly argues that the modern age does not have merely one point of origin, which came about in the seventeenth century as the result of a series of rather smooth and predictable historical developments, but actually two. The first beginning occurred 100 to 150 years earlier in the Renaissance, which, Toulmin argues, was the literary or humanistic phase of the modern age. The second beginning, the only one seen by the standard account, is what he calls the scientific and philosophical phase – which from 1630 led Europeans to turn their backs on the most potent themes of the literary, humanistic phase.[5]

He attributes this abrupt departure from the modern age's first beginning to the profound social and political unrest that swept across Europe at the beginning of the seventeenth century, particularly the Thirty Years' War (1618–48). Thinkers in the seventeenth century were caught in a world that was embroiled in conflict – conflict that resulted, in large measure, from the inability of Catholics and Protestants to reconcile their rival theological positions. The task at hand for these thinkers was to discover a more cool-headed and humane way to settle these disputes. They found little help from their sixteenth-century predecessors, who had reveled in paradoxical points of view and exotic, alternative ways of life. These seventeenth-century thinkers embarked instead on a quest to discover a way to know what could be known *with certainty*. They did so by conceiving of *objective, universal, timeless knowledge* that is untainted by human subjectivity and accessed by the proper use of reason or rationality. As a result they essentially turned the practical knowledge of the Renaissance on its head, stressing instead the importance of the written over the oral, the universal over the particular, the general over the local, and the timeless over the timely.[6]

The real genius of Toulmin's thesis is in how he applies these observations about the modern age's two beginnings to our present-day situation. He notes that by the latter half of the twentieth century the major themes of the modern age's second beginning – its scientific, philosophical phase – started to lose influence. This in turn allowed the themes of the modern age's first beginning – its literary, humanistic phase, which lay submerged for almost 400 years – to bubble back to the surface. In other words, what we are witnessing today in both the cultural and philosophical manifestations of postmodernism is a resurgence of the modern age's first beginning. Thus it might be fair to say that, in some sense at least, we are living in a "resurgent age" as much as an "emergent age"; a "most-modern era" as much as a "postmodern era."

The real point of all this is that when modern Christians and postmodern Christians draw lines between each other, they do so primarily because of disagreements about the nature of knowledge. Modern Christians appeal to the "basic beliefs" model. For them the nature of truth is joined at the hip with their conception of knowledge. When postmodern Christians insist that there's no such thing as basic beliefs, they are, in the modern Christians' view, denying the existence of absolute truth. Rather than dismissing these concerns as antiquated and irrelevant, postmodern Christians would do well to grapple more deeply with how best to express their belief in God's Truth that is at once transcendent (and therefore *not socially constructed*) and immanent (and thus *socially comprehended*).

Better yet, given our common participation in things modern, we would do best to stop drawing lines between ourselves altogether and together look for another way to conceive of and experience the truth of Christ.

Robert and the French Fry

I bring this rather dense reflection on knowledge to a close by coming full circle and recounting one of the most meaningful experiences that I had as a doctoral student at Fuller Seminary. It was not the result of my interaction with one of Fuller's many elite, world-class professors. Nor did it come through the "simple meals" at Jim and Nancey's house, or my interaction with fellow students, or my own scholarly reflection. The most memorable and personally formative experience came from the unlikeliest of people at Fuller Seminary – from a disabled man named Robert. I met Robert under the most awkward of circumstances. He approached me while I was by myself at the Refectory, the main dining hall at Fuller. I was preparing to enjoy a hamburger and fries. I was halfway through the first term of studies and in the grip of research and writing. I had also just assumed a new role as senior pastor of a thriving church in San Diego county – this on top of my responsibilities as a husband and father of three young children. My commute to school was 140 miles each way, and I was doing it twice a week at that point. It was all I could do to keep my sanity.

I had noticed Robert on several occasions, always sitting in the Garth, a plaza located at the center of student life and activity – between the library, classrooms, and school eateries. I wondered what brought him to the campus. It was clear that he suffered from a debilitating abnormality that rendered him besotted. He staggered when he walked and slurred conspicuously when he spoke. He seemed harmless enough, interacting cordially with the students that happened to be milling about the plaza, but I kept my distance. I surmised that he might be related to one of the school's employees. I had just paid for my meal and sat down at an empty table near the window to savor a juicy hamburger and thick-cut fries. It was a much-needed respite between early morning class, a long day of research at the library, and the equally wearisome drive through southern California traffic still ahead.

I felt Robert's eyes on me as I made my way to the table. He seemed to be studying me. No sooner had I settled into my seat than he got up and started walking in my direction. "Oh great," I thought. "What does this guy want?" Robert approached and politely asked if he could join me. "So much for solitude," I muttered under my breath. "Sure, have a seat," I answered, smiling fraudulently. As soon as he sat down he asked for a fry. "Okay, now I know why he came over," I mused sarcastically. "He's looking for a handout. I was wrong. He's not the relative of an employee. He's a local bum who's learned that it pays to prey on the kindness of seminary students." My default in such situations is kindness rather than open disdain, so I told him to help himself. I was in for a lesson that would change me forever.

Robert insisted that I feed him the fry. The request jolted me, but I quickly recovered, guessing that his disability limited his hand–eye coordination. I asked if he wanted me to dip the fry in ketchup. "Oh, yes thank you," he said. It felt strange to hand feed a full-grown man who was at least ten years my senior. I wondered who else in the room might be watching this unusual occurrence. When Robert thanked me, I thought that might be the end of it – but it was not. Without asking he picked up another fry and dipped it in the ketchup. The thought that immediately struck me was, "This guy's playing with my mind. He didn't need my help to eat that fry. Now he's making me look like a fool for going along with his request." Then Robert did the unthinkable. Holding up the ketchup-covered fry, in eucharistic pose, he looked straight into my eyes and said, "Now I want to feed you."

My face flushed with embarrassment. "What are the other people here going to think *now*?" I worried. Reluctantly I consented to this befuddling gesture and received the chip into my mouth. He reached for another while he spoke. "When my mom was in labor with me, there was an umbilical cord prolapse. Do you know what that is?" After a slight pause he answered his own question. "It's when the cord gets caught in the birth canal as the baby is trying to pass through, cutting off its blood and oxygen." Robert's hand swayed noticeably as he raised the second fry to my mouth. I rocked my head from side to side to intercept it between my teeth without getting smudged with ketchup. He continued, "I was a blue baby when I was born. The doctors say I went without oxygen for over four minutes." My throat tightened as he continued to speak, making it difficult to swallow. "I didn't start walking until I was nine years old. I couldn't dress myself or feed myself until I was in my twenties. And I still can't bathe or go to the bathroom by myself."

I cleared my throat with a gulp of diet Coke as Robert dipped another fry in ketchup. But he held it, unsteadily, off to the side. "I want to ask you something personal," he said, tilting his head to the right. The ketchup-covered fry wavered back and forth in an erratic, undulating motion. "Go ahead," I answered. He leaned forward and slid the morsel into my mouth, "Do you realize how blessed you are? Have you ever stopped yourself in the morning before you get out of bed to say, 'Thank you so much, God, that I am able to get up without anybody's help'? Do you ever thank him for being able to bathe and go to the bathroom alone, or to dress yourself and feed yourself?"

I admitted that I scarcely paid much attention to such matters, "No, not really . . . not the way I should," I said sheepishly. Then he reached down and took hold of my knees as if to turn me away from the table and toward him,

"Here, turn your chair and face me." I scooted back from the table and rotated my seat. He edged his chair as close to me as he could get it. We sat face to face, our knees touching. He reached toward me, offering both hands to mine, saying, "I want to pray with you." I was no longer concerned about what others in the dining hall thought of our unusual conversation. In fact I was no longer aware of anyone else at all. I grasped his hands with upturned palms to help steady him as he prayed. We closed our eyes and leaned forward. Our heads were almost touching.

He prayed, "Lord, I thank you for my new friend, Chuck, and for letting me have some of his French fries." I cried silently, "Forgive me, O God, for my judgmental and selfish spirit." Robert continued without interruption, "Thank you for blessing Chuck with so many gifts – he can feed himself and dress himself. Thank you that he doesn't need anyone else's help to wash or go to the bathroom. Please help him to enjoy these gifts and to celebrate the fact that they come from you. Amen."

I answered with a corresponding "Amen." Thinking that we were finished, I lightened my hold on his hands to signal as much, but he held his grip, "Now I want you to pray and to thank God for these blessings." I glanced up to see if he was serious. His body was still and steady, and he smiled softly. The gaze of his greenish-brown eyes reached all the way to my soul. I had no choice but to comply. Robert had essentially given me the script. All I had to do was pray what he prayed. It felt strange to do so, but, drawing from my pastoral expertise, I proceeded: "God, thank you for bringing Robert to my table this afternoon. His story reminds me that I often overlook the most basic blessings of all. Thank you for giving me the ability to get out of bed in the morning. Thank you as well that I do not need anybody's help to bathe or dress or eat or go to the bathroom."

After I finished praying, Robert leaned forward and hugged me. He thanked me for welcoming him to my table. Then he excused himself and left the dining hall through the front door. I returned to my now-lukewarm hamburger as he shuffled across the courtyard and sat down by the large,

square planter box at the center of the plaza. It was filled
with a lush array of pansies and petunias that danced in solid
and variegated shades of white, purple, pink, red, yellow,
and blue. The colors had begun to pale under the dusk sky.
Robert sat alone. His arms, crossed, rested in his lap. His lips
were moving – as though he was talking to himself or to
God – and he was rocking back and forth ever so slightly.

All at once I realized who Robert was and why he was at
Fuller Seminary. This was his ministry . . . his calling. God
had placed him here, in the middle of this bustling world
of higher Christian education, to awaken as many of us as
possible to the truth that we are not creatures of our own
making. We are not nearly as wise as we think we are, and
all the knowledge we're getting from this place is nothing
but dry bones without the life-giving breath of God. What
matters is not what we make of ourselves by means of
theological education or by any other human effort. The only
thing that matters is what God makes of us . . . and God can
make anything out of anybody he chooses. In this case, he
had made of Robert – a forty-five-year-old social outcast who
could neither bathe nor defecate without help of others – an
angel of mercy, the perfect messenger to would-be educated
elites. And his message for us is one of the most important
truths of all – it is our love for God and not our acquisition
of knowledge that builds up the body of Christ and draws
us into ever greater intimacy with the One who makes of us
what he pleases.

Knowledge puffs up, but love builds up. Those who think
they know something do not yet know as they ought to know.
But those who love God are known by God." (1 Corinthians
8:1–3, TNIV)

8. Beyond All Reasonable Doubt

The heavens declare the glory of God; the skies proclaim the work of his hands. Day after day they pour forth speech; night after night they display knowledge. There is no speech or language where their voice is not heard. Their voice goes out into all the earth, their words to the ends of the world.

Psalm 19:1–4

I don't believe I will ever walk away from God for intellectual reasons. Who knows anything anyway? If I walk away from Him, and please pray that I never do, I will walk away for social reasons, identity reasons, deep emotional reasons, the same reasons that any of us do anything.
Donald Miller, *Blue Like Jazz*

Nature's Revelation of God

Nature attests to God's diversity. There are over 9,500 documented species of birds,[1] and more than 250,000 species of flowering plants – to say nothing of all other plant life. And researchers who have tried to come up with a reasonable estimate of microorganisms and their respective types have been forced to conclude that it is impossible even to venture a guess – other than to say it's like trying to count the stars in the universe.

Of course diversity can be appreciated in other ways besides raw numbers. Nature displays the wonder and playfulness of God. From giraffes to gerbils to goats and geese; from kangaroos to koalas to quails and whales; from pandas to porcupines to porpoises and pachyderms, God's enjoyment of variety is on display for all to see. There's the industrious teamwork of ants, and the solitary labor of the spider that meticulously weaves its web and waits in stillness for its prey. Penguins survive the harshest of Antarctic conditions by means of extraordinarily ordered community. Nature, in other words, provides ample evidence that there's a lot more to God than meets the eye. Being mindful of our surroundings is all it takes for us to appreciate the fact that the One who made our world delights in paradox and mystery.

Knowledge Explosion and the Decline of Christian Spirituality

In the light of our surroundings, it makes little sense to assume that we have the capacity to comprehend truth in its fullness – and to be absolutely certain about that fact. As we observed in the last chapter, the need we often feel to "get it right" when it comes to divine truth is the legacy of our seventeenth-century brothers and sisters who did their best to live faithfully in a world embroiled in religious conflict. There is admittedly a certain comfort in distinguishing between what's true and what's false, what's right and what's wrong, and who's in and who's out. But we must ask at what cost we carry on this way. And if there were ever a time in history when we could feel confident about "knowing what we know," it is now. We can research subjects at lightening speed. Information that used to take weeks or months to collect can now be gathered in a single afternoon. The Internet is arguably the greatest step forward in putting the whole world at our fingertips.

We can compare the emergence of the Internet to the invention of the printing press over 550 years ago. The mass production of reading material not only made it easier to transmit existing forms of information, but also opened up a world of new possibilities. The Protestant Reformation movements were carried on the wings of the age of print. For example, the ninety-five theses that Luther nailed to the front door of the Wittenberg Cathedral were penned in Latin, and therefore inaccessible to most churchgoing Germans. But an enterprising individual translated Luther's words into German and mass-produced them on the printing press. Had it not been for this new technology, so-called Protestantism might have never gotten off the ground.

In bringing information to the masses in forms and quantities never before imagined, the printing press actually changed the way we think. In the past, communities were largely non-literate.[2] The stories they passed on from one generation to the next were their *stories of identity*. They were communicated orally and remembered word for word. These stories gave the people in non-literate cultures a shared understanding of their past and present world. In some instances, a community's history was preserved in writing, but the prevailing norm was oral tradition, which was safeguarded in memory and passed along to future generations by word of mouth.

As more people learned how to read, several monumental shifts eventually occurred. For one, most who embraced this new technology were the community's younger members, which led to the same phenomenon that we are experiencing today as "the digital divide." Young people became much less dependent on their communities – particularly the aged members of their communities – for their information. Additionally, these new readers – basking as they were in the warm light of the latest and greatest information – identified less and less with their own stories of identity. Eventually the world became a place in which individuals trumped community and youth triumphed over age.

A growing number of experts claim that the Internet has put us on the threshold of an information renaissance comparable to that of the printing press, bringing with it the same potential to change our social structures. Not surprisingly, many churches and faith-based organizations have mounted efforts to further the work of Christ through the Internet. David McDonald, citing the recent Pew Internet and American Life Project, observes that 21 percent of Internet users search the web for what he calls "cyber spiritual connection," making online spirituality more popular than online banking (18 percent) or online auctions (15 percent).[3]

Nevertheless, even though the Internet gives us access to literally thousands of different sources for spiritual growth, statisticians have observed a steady cooling of our spiritual passions over the last several years, showing that the accessibility of information in itself is not the only resource needed for spiritual development." One study conducted a few years ago by the Barna Research Group Ltd – an organization that routinely examines the religious condition of contemporary culture – witnessed a "statistically significant change" from 1991 to 2001 in four of seven measures used to assess spiritual health among professing believers. George Barna, the Group's founder, believes that these statistics suggest that we are stuck in a deep rut.[5] While online resources and Internet use have exploded over the past several years, our spiritual vitality has actually waned.

The reason that the Internet has not been more effective in forming us spiritually is because the majority of faith-based organizations have yet to make the most of the growing trend toward cyber spiritual community. A small but growing number seem to be catching on, but there are still many Christian communities that use the Internet as a glorified, digital file cabinet, giving members and would-be seekers access to information about the worship services, small group offerings, and directions to the building. More sophisticated websites may even include the pastor's sermons in downloadable form. For all its effectiveness in connecting us to an endless array of valuable information, the Internet's potential to foster redemptive community is often ignored – which at the end of the day is "the missing link" in terms of enhancing our spiritual vitality. Churches and other religious groups would do well to look for web providers that can help them transform their websites from repositories of information to places of social engagement and community building.

I was contacted recently by the representative of a company that produces state-of-the-art websites for churches. He found out that I teach a seminary course in which I require my students to investigate various church software companies and present their findings in class. He wanted to come and demonstrate his product to my students and I agreed to let him do so. His presentation was thorough and professional. However, for all its bells and whistles, the website that his company provides does not have a single feature for community building. When my students kindly pointed out this deficiency, the sales representative responded by saying that the company may eventually get around to adding such features, but he said it did not consider this a priority. And the reason that most church website companies do not consider community-building functions a priority is because *most churches* do not consider them a priority, demonstrating the widespread problem that we cannot seem to shake. We are stuck in an information rut.

It is worth noting that the church played a major role in shaping Western civilization's educational landscape from the medieval period through the last century.[6] In this sense the church's preoccupation with information is not new. What is different now, however, is how the church's emphasis on information has taken center stage. Christians in the last century have been more consumed with *getting correct information* (i.e., "truth") than with acting justly, loving mercy, and walking humbly with God (Micah 6:8). While this attraction to knowledge first affected Christian theologians in the seventeenth and eighteenth centuries, the resulting trickle-down effect has influenced our experiences of personal and corporate spirituality ever since.

Two Approaches to Christian Spirituality

We have inherited from the seventeenth century two primary approaches to Christian spirituality: *the way of knowledge* and its reactionary counterpart, *the way of piety*. The result of both approaches is the same: we tend to construe our spirituality in very black-and-white terms – either as the accumulation of knowledge or the acquisition of virtue. In either case, spiritual growth is viewed as something that we achieve through our own effort and for our own personal benefit. The themes of knowledge and piety are not mutually exclusive, of course. Most would say that one very naturally leads to or complements the other. But neither approach, even when taken with the other, provides an adequate way to achieve spiritual growth.

The way of knowledge

For all the benefits bequeathed to us by the intellectual strides of the past 500 years,[7] a significant downside has been the tendency to conceive of spirituality in terms of accumulating religious knowledge. Such knowledge *may* prove helpful to one's growth in the life of the Spirit, but not always. We do well to remember that it was the biblically and theologically educated people in the first century that most violently opposed Jesus and, afterward, the expansion of the early church. Jesus observed that the educated elite of his day diligently studied Scripture because they believed the knowledge gained through that effort would bring eternal life. In the end, however, their knowledge actually prevented them from recognizing their Messiah when he was standing right in front of them (see John 5:39, 40).

Two great thinkers, St. Augustine and St. Anselm, reminded us long ago that knowledge is not an end itself. It is simply a means to deepen our faith. Both men emphasized the priority of faith over knowledge, recognizing that there is a big difference between *knowledge of spiritual things* and *spiritual mindedness.*[8] Scripture speaks much more about the need to be spiritually minded than to be spiritually knowledgeable. When the Apostle Paul calls us to be renewed in the spirit of our minds (Ephesians 4:23) and to be transformed by the renewing of our minds (Romans 12:1, 2), he is describing a state in which the sum of our mental energies is concentrated on and taken up in the very life of God. In this way we love God with "the entire mind" (Mark 12:30).

In the past several hundred years much undue emphasis was placed on the value of our individual knowledge as the path to spiritual enlightenment. "Discipleship" in the twentieth century was seen more along the lines of *the transmission of information* than *the transformation of our character.* Of course no present-day advocate of discipleship would say that knowledge is to be preferred over a transformed life. The assumption instead is that knowledge quite naturally leads us into the transformed life.[9] At face value this conviction does not seem out of step with the biblical mandate to be transformed by the renewing of the mind, but its inadequacy can be assessed in terms of the simple fact that "disciples" in the biblical sense are typically not produced. This has prompted people like Jim Petersen to lament, "Thirty years of discipleship programs and we are still not discipled!"[10]

The way of piety

By the latter part of the seventeenth century a German church leader named Philipp Jakob Spener (b. 1635) was convinced that Protestant orthodoxy, with its emphasis on right thinking over right living, had missed the mark. Spener concluded that preaching and church attendance alone were inadequate to sustain spiritual vitality. So he gathered small groups of disciples and had them focus on six overlapping aspects of the Christian life that he believed most Catholics and Protestants were ignoring at the time: (1) a more thorough acquaintance with Scripture; (2) the universal priesthood of all believers; (3) the balancing of spiritual knowledge with the practice of charity and forgiveness; (4) bringing unbelievers to faith; (5) theological reflection that was not merely expounded but exemplified in good works; and (6) preaching that stressed faith and right living instead of polished rhetoric. Out of those early meetings another movement was born – pietism.

Pietism has gained many adherents over the last several hundred years and has had a powerful influence on the formation of many faith communities in Europe, North America, and beyond. It has provided a much-needed counterbalance to the sterile intellectualism of the Age of Reason. But there is also a dark side – namely, the tendency to put too much stress on godly behavior, which is defined for the most part in negative terms. "I don't smoke; I don't chew, and I don't go with girls that do," is a popular and admittedly humorous expression of pietism. Personal holiness is construed in light of what we have to overcome. The main focus, in other words, is on all the things *we shouldn't be doing*. Such holiness lists are as telling for what they omit as for what they include. Gambling, for example, makes almost every holiness list, but gossip typically does not. Alcohol and tobacco usually top the list of forbidden fruits, while the excessive consumption of hamburgers and ice cream – which is responsible for more heart attacks and strokes than alcohol and tobacco combined – is conspicuously absent.

Few would argue that attributes of a godly character – such as the ones identified by the Apostle Paul as the *fruit* (not fruits) of the Spirit: "love, joy, peace, patience, kindness, goodness, faithfulness, gentleness, and self-control" (Galatians 5:22, 23) – are well worth pursuing. However, we put the theological cart before the horse when we insist that the way to attain spiritual maturity is by pursuing these attributes as ends in themselves. In fact, the apostle is seeking to make *the opposite* point in this passage. The Holy Spirit produces this fruit in the lives of those who are rightly related to Jesus Christ. Fruit is not the *means* of spiritual growth; it is the *product* of a relationship with Christ that is fostered and sustained by the Spirit.

The problem with both these approaches – the way of knowledge and the way of piety – is that we attempt to measure the quality of our spirituality in black-and-white terms: either by what we know or by what we do (and do not do).

The Bizarre Behavior of Black-and-White Thinking

Black-and-white thinking gets us into all kinds of trouble, especially when we apply it to the things of God. Historically, it has made Christians do some wacky and horrendous things. It led sixteenth-century Swiss reformer, Ulrich Zwingli, to go so far as to say that Christians should not use any part of their bodies in worship – including their voices in singing, since the Apostle Paul said that we are to "sing and make melody *with our hearts* to the Lord." It led Catholics and Protestants alike to brutally persecute Anabaptists, who adopted the novel concept (novel to their persecutors at least) that the church in its purest form consists only of believers. It led the Catholic Church to imprison Galileo for the "heretical teaching" that the earth moves around the sun.[11] It led Massachusetts Puritans to launch an inquisition, remembered as the Salem witch hunts, that filled their prisons with innocent people and incited the townspeople to execute at least twenty-five. And that's just a few examples from the sixteenth and seventeenth centuries. Black-and-white thinking continues to exact a costly toll on followers of Christ.

Sometimes when I introduce myself to strangers they associate me with Chuck Conners, the star of the black-and-white TV western, *The Rifleman*, which aired from 1958 to 1963. "Oh, you're the *rifleman*?" they will say kiddingly. (I'm much too young to have appeared on that show in any form other than a small child.) While I do not mind being identified with the likes of Conners, who sported a Winchester rifle with its trademark rapid-fire trigger mechanism, I would recoil at the prospect of being associated with the rifleman in the following story.

A non-denominational congregation in the Midwest had recently purchased the town's historic Congregational Church building, which had stood as the community's centerpiece for over a hundred years. Its grounds were expertly manicured. Expansive carpets of lush, green grass encircled cobblestone walkways and award-winning rose bushes – several of which, according to local folklore, had been planted a century before by the town's founding fathers and mothers. Several large oak trees were purposefully stationed across the property to provide ample shade for locals and visitors reclining on the grass with blankets or sitting on one of the black iron benches nestled amid white marble birdbaths and clusters of red and white tulips and yellow daffodils.

The building itself was a large, cathedral-like structure made of gray stone blocks, fine wood, and colorful stained glass windows. The dark brown double wooden doors at the front of the building were said to have been salvaged from the ruins of an ancient church in Turkey. Its towering steeple and cross could be seen from all points north, south, east, and west. The interior walls of the nave were adorned with beautiful floor-to-ceiling frescos depicting various scenes from Jesus' life and passion. So far as the townspeople were concerned, the church building and its grounds was the community's crown jewel.

The new occupants of this monument, however, were scarcely impressed with the building's rich history and aesthetics. The congregation embraced a black-and-white approach to Scripture that was quite similar to that of Ulrich Zwingli. They believed that the pictures reflected in the stained glass windows and frescos were tantamount to the graven images condemned in the Ten Commandments. Although they did not disclose their intentions to the former owners when they purchased the structure, the group planned to carry out sweeping renovations to expunge the building of any and every trace of such idolatry.

The group had been meeting in their new surroundings for less than a month. Several of the church's leading men had just finished their first Saturday morning men's breakfast. The conversation that morning focused on the question of whether they should remove the stained glass windows and the wall frescos and sell them to another group or destroy them altogether – "since these images are in fact an abomination to God." Although they acknowledged that the windows and frescos were priceless works of art, they reasoned that if they sold these artifacts to another group, it would be the same as approving of their profane use. The works of art had to be destroyed. The stained glass windows would be removed and demolished and the wall frescos would be painted over.

But what to do with the cross atop the towering steeple outside? They concluded that it too had to go. But how? The men eyed the cross from the parking lot on the south side of the building. To scale the soaring spire would be to risk life and limb. And it would be stiflingly cost prohibitive to hire a crane to remove the fixture. One of the men spoke up, "I think I know how to get that thing down." His name was Harvey. He was wearing blue jean overalls, a tattered white T-shirt, and a green and black camouflage hunting cap. "Won't cost but a nickel," he continued. The men knew Harvey well enough to discern what he was proposing. They smiled at each other and gave him an approving nod.

Harvey got into his dilapidated, navy blue '68 Ford pickup and sputtered around to the front of the building where he parked on the street. He got out of the vehicle and stood between the cab and open driver's door. Then he removed a large-caliber hunting rifle – complete with a high-powered scope – from the gun rack mounted on the inside back window. Using the roof of the cab to steady his aim, Harvey positioned the weapon. The men ran around the side of the building to get a better look. They were laughing and slapping each other on the back, half disbelieving and half delighting in what was about to happen.

Harvey peered through the scope, bringing the base of the massive wooden cross into the crosshairs. Gently he squeezed the trigger. The large firearm discharged with a thundering explosion. Windows of nearby homes rattled and the flock of chick-a-dees roosting in the church's largest oak tree scattered in a fluttering, hysterical frenzy. Heads turned from every direction – the mother pushing her infant daughter in a baby carriage; the retired school teacher, tending her garden in the mild mid-morning sun. Lawnmowers ceased their mowing and townsfolk young and old bolted outside to see what had stolen the tranquility of their Saturday morning.

All eyes and ears were fixed on the center of town. The 300-pound cross was mortally wounded. To the dismay of dozens of horrified onlookers, the cruciform troubadour twisted in a counterclockwise motion, as if to stretch its right hand to an adoring crowd – and with the creaking and snapping of the last strained timbers, it gave its final bow and plummeted, headfirst, to the cobblestone sidewalk below. It landed with such force that it shattered in two, launching the crossbeam into a tumble that ended at the north entry of the narthex. The thud was felt in the chests of all who witnessed this surreal event.

In minutes the local sheriff arrived at the scene. With red and blue lights flashing, he angled his cruiser in front of

Harvey's truck to prevent any attempts at a speedy getaway. Dozens of stunned citizens gathered in the sidewalks that surrounded the now-marred monument. Two boys rode their bicycles onto the church property to get an up-close look at the dismembered cross. Passing cars slowed to a stop as more and more community members tried to make out what had just happened.

Only then did the men of that congregation realize the reckless and ill-fated nature of this display. Sirens screamed from every direction as the rest of the town's emergency personnel descended on the scene. Two other police units came screeching to a halt. The fire truck and paramedics came next. Two reporters and one photographer from the local newspaper got there shortly after that. The fire chief showed up last – his fishing pole sticking out the passenger window with the worm and bobber dangling against the outside of the door. The first police officer on the scene handcuffed Harvey and put him in the back of his patrol car. He arrested him for discharging a firearm within city limits.

"What kind of crazed lunatic would have done such a thing?" the people wondered. No one who lived in the town – aside from the members of that congregation – could have imagined that a man professing to be a follower of Jesus Christ would shoot the cross off his own church . . . and that with the unanimous support of the church's leading men.

It did not take long for word to spread that it was actually several members of the church who had schemed to destroy the historic cross. The event made Sunday morning headlines. Amazingly, when queried by one of the two reporters, the men of the congregation defended Harvey's actions. They informed the newspaper that the cross, along with the stained glass windows and wall frescos were offensive to God and had to be removed from the premises forthwith.

The news sent shockwaves through the town. That week an emergency session of the city council was convened and "a historic landmarks commission" was promptly created. The commission in turn made a formal recommendation to the council that the church and its grounds be designated a historic landmark by local ordinance. A press release saying as much was published and a town hall was called to determine whether the community supported the commission's proposal. On the night of the meeting city hall had never been so crowded. It was a media circus. News agencies across the state sent reporters, television crews, and local radio personalities to cover the proceedings.

The event was emotionally charged to say the least. Irate townsfolk expressed rage and hostility toward the eccentric occupants of their local treasure. One of the church's elders tried to object to the commission's proposal on grounds that it violated the church's religious freedom, but he was drowned out by the shouts of the angry mob. After several grueling hours of community input, the city council passed an ordinance that designated the church and its grounds a historic landmark, thereby compelling its owners, under threat of severe penalties, to preserve and maintain the property's important historic features. The council further ordered the occupants of the landmark to restore the cross atop the steeple to its original state.

Faced with what they deemed an impossible situation, the congregation sold the property to the town's newly established historical society and vacated the premises – never again to have a presence in that community.

Black-and-white thinking may not drive all of us to shoot the crosses off our church buildings – not literally at least. But in almost every instance it displaces the cross of Christ by reducing the wonder and mystery of God's ways to intellectual and behavioral formulae. In the next several chapters we consider another alternative to the way of knowledge and the way of piety. It too has its roots in the seventeenth century – though its origins go much deeper into antiquity than that. This third way may well mark the path that followers of Christ must now take if they hope to soar in the Spirit.

9. A New Creation!

The coming of the kingdom of God is not something that can be observed, nor will people say, "Here it is," or "There it is," because the kingdom of God is in your midst.

Luke 17:21, TNIV

O God, since Thou art with me, and it is Thy will that I must now apply myself to these outward duties, I beseech Thee, assist me with Thy grace that I may continue in Thy presence. To this end, O Lord, be with me in this my work, accept the labor of my hands, and dwell within my heart with all Thy fullness.

Brother Lawrence, *The Practice of the Presence of God*

Heaven's Kitchen

Seventeenth-century Europe was a time and place of tortured upheaval and change. After the dust settled on the Thirty Years War (1618–48) nothing would ever be the same. There was no returning to the idealism and exuberance of the Renaissance, by then a hundred years forgotten. Though few at the time would have ventured to give it a name, they had entered the Age of Reason where coolheaded thinkers like philosopher and mathematician René Descartes ruled the day. Christian theology was now "a thinking man's game." European Christians who didn't like the intellectualizing of their faith eventually had another option at their disposal – the pietistic program developed by German church leader,

Philipp Jakob Spener. The development of Protestantism in the centuries that followed was complex, to put it mildly. But, for the most part, the "way of knowledge" and the "way of piety" – the traditions represented by Descartes and Spener, respectively – emerged as the two principal conduits of Christian life and thought. For the most part, that is.

There were other seventeenth-century voices that spoke of a way besides that of knowledge and piety – the voices of people like George Fox, Madame Guyon, and Miguel de Molinos. Their concerns and experiences tended to differ markedly from those of their fellow rationalists and pietists. They emerged in different places and circumstances and were not unified by any overarching society or formal union. Yet they described a common set of experiences that made it clear they were cut from the same cloth. They are the "mystics." Whereas the rationalists were consumed with "orthodoxy" (the right teaching) and the pietists with "orthopraxy" (the right behavior), the mystics were absorbed in what we might call "Christopraxis" (the Christ-life). Mystics, in other words, would never dream of asking, "What would Jesus do?" (Much less wear a WWJD T-shirt or bracelet.) The question betrays a deadly theological assumption, which is brought to light by finishing the question: "What would Jesus do *if he were actually here*?"

What distinguishes mystics from their rationalistic and pietistic counterparts is, for lack of a better way of saying it, a sustained experience of God's presence. The Apostle Paul may well be considered one of the first Christian mystics when he makes statements like, "I have been crucified with Christ and I no longer live, but Christ lives in me" (Galatians 2:20) and ". . . for it is God who works in you to will and to act according to his good purpose" (Philippians 2:13). For mystics, God is not to be found in rationalistic propositions or pietistic practices, for such things are of our own making. God is encountered in the immediacy of daily life.

Of all the seventeenth-century spiritual luminaries, none shines brighter than Brother Lawrence, a lowly monastery kitchen aide who spent his days in relative obscurity, clearing table scraps, washing dishes, and mopping floors. At birth his peasant parents named him Nicholas Herman. He spent his childhood in Lorraine, France. In his late teens poverty drove him to join the army. During his military service Nicholas had an awakening that sensitized him to the things of the Spirit as never before. It was a cold winter day and he had been in an emotional trough that left him feeling dead inside. As he gazed at a leafless tree he was overcome with the wonder of God's presence. Just as the barren tree waited silently and patiently for the new life that spring would surely bring, Nicholas knew in that instant that God had new life waiting for him. What grew in his soul from that point on was not so much a supernatural vision of God's presence as it was an extraordinary clarity of ordinary perception. An injury forced Nicholas to leave the army sometime later and eventually he entered the Discalced Carmelite monastery in Paris, assuming the name Brother Lawrence.

Brother Lawrence's days were spent as an underling in the monastery kitchen where he was forever at the beck and call of his superiors. Yet it was in this crucible of the mundane that Brother Lawrence forged an extraordinary consciousness of God's presence. For this saint the clamor and clatter of the kitchen were no less the sacramental objects of Christ's presence than the Eucharist itself. "The time of business," said Lawrence, "does not with me differ from the time of prayer, and in the noise and clatter of my kitchen, while several persons are at the same time calling for different things, I possess God as if I were upon my knees at the blessed sacrament."[1]

Brother Lawrence believed that when we invent "means and methods" of coming at God's love, and "learn rules and devices" to remind us of that love, we make it all the more difficult – "a world of trouble," as he put it – to sustain our awareness of God's presence. He was convinced that the primary medium through which God is present to us is the "common business" of life. It is not necessary to do great things, he said. We can do little things for God:

> I turn the cake that is frying on the pan for love of him, and
> that done, if there is nothing else to call me, I prostrate myself

in worship before him, who has given me grace to work; afterwards I rise happier than a king. It is enough for me to pick up but a straw from the ground for the love of God.[2]

Brother Lawrence's "practice of the presence of God," as it came to be known, is descriptive of a common phenomenon among mystics – an experience of the all-encompassing immediacy of God's presence in the most ordinary, even debasing of circumstances. Twentieth-century mystic Mother Teresa expresses the same sense of Christ's presence. When she served the poor as she did so faithfully, she was not serving them *on behalf of* Christ. She was serving Christ himself in his "distressing disguise":

> The more repugnant the work, or the more disfigured or deformed the image of God in the person, the greater will be our faith and loving devotion in seeking the face of Jesus, and lovingly ministering to him in his distressing disguise. We need to realize that we have the privilege of touching Jesus twenty-four hours a day. When I'm feeding that child, I'm feeding Jesus. These poor people are Jesus suffering today. If we want the poor to see Christ in us, we must first see Christ in the poor.[3]

For Brother Lawrence it was the commotion and demands of life in a monastery kitchen that sacramentally conveyed Christ's presence as in the Eucharist. For Mother Teresa it was the stinking, decomposing flesh of Calcutta's leper-ridden untouchables. "When I touch the smelling body," she said, "I know I touch the body of Christ as I receive Him in the Holy Communion under the sign of bread."

Christ is all around us, adorned in the limitless disguises of daily life. For most of us, like Brother Lawrence, this realization comes in at least two ways – in the form of spiritual aha! moments, barren tree experiences, when at once all things become new in some way, and by means of spiritual discipline that slowly, haltingly, failingly at times, brings us to a state of heightened spiritual awareness. Some of us experience an initial aha! moment at the time of conversion. For others, like John Wesley, it comes sometime later. Most disciples experience several such awakenings in their lives.

The Apostle Paul appears to be describing this aha! experience in 2 Corinthians 5. The majority of English translations put it this way: "If anyone is in Christ, he is a new creation! The old has gone, the new has come!" (2 Corinthians 5:17). But this is to miss the real point that the apostle is making. Paul does not mean to say that the newly awakened disciple is him- or herself a new creation – not in this passage at least. He means to convey that *our world becomes new to us* at the moment of awakening. As a despairing Nicholas Herman stared at the barren tree, scales fell from his eyes and he could never again look at a leafless tree – or see any other tree – the same way. His world was new. The phrase, *"a new creation!"* in this passage is the exclamation that bursts forth at the moment of spiritual awakening. The translators of both the NRSV and TNIV correctly capture the nuance of Paul's point: "If anyone is in Christ . . . *a new creation!*" It's a flash of mystery – the aha!

The lives of most followers of Jesus Christ are punctuated by these flashes of mystery. They are few and far between for most of us, but they are unforgettable. The first aha! moment came for me at an early age when my mother took the crucifix from the wall and showed me that God was nailed to a cross. The potato chip incident, which I described earlier, was a new-creation moment as well. Another flash of mystery occurred at age twenty when God showed up as the disquieting intruder, announcing that the choice to live or die was mine – and again six months later, when my piano teacher, Merriam, shared the good news that flooded my soul with life-giving water. My experience with Robert and the French fries opened my eyes to yet another facet of God's mystery. There have been several others. While these experiences are different, they share a common quality that strikes with déjà-vu-like familiarity.

New creation moments are significant events that often mark a passage from one chapter of our spiritual journey to the next. They are God's touches – sometimes frightening, sometimes comforting; sometimes constructive, sometimes reconstructive. In some cases those around us perceive little if anything different about us. But in every instance these significant events change us in some way. They may be turning points, moments of confirmation, or alterations of our paradigm. At times people experience these awakenings in groups. Retreats and revivals typically serve as venues for such experiences. In other cases whole families undergo new-creation experiences, as was the case in the New Testament's story of the Philippian jailor and his family (see Acts 16:16–40).

Several years ago my family and I experienced a profoundly memorable significant event during a stressful transition period. After twelve years of life-enriching fellowship with my denomination – the group that had played so pivotal a role in my spiritual formation after I left Roman Catholicism – I found myself at a theological impasse. Experience has taught me that most of the time when people say they're leaving a fellowship for theological reasons, they are kidding themselves. However, more than twenty years later – and after much soul searching – I believe the problem in this case was in fact theological.

The denomination I'm speaking of has two distinguishing peculiarities. For one, they insist that the New Testament does not authorize the use of instrumental music in gathered Christian worship. By "authorize" they mean that there is no record in the New Testament of "mechanical instruments of music" being used or approved for worship – and the absence of any specific command or example means for them that the use of instruments is thereby forbidden.

I started to question my fellowship's position on instrumental music in my fourth year of pastoral ministry. It did not help matters that I was attending a seminary of another denomination, which approved of musical instruments in worship. I was serving as an associate minister at the time and had enjoyed a cordial relationship with the senior minister. We often spent time in each other's offices talking openly about our dreams and struggles. So it did not seem out of place to bring up my wrestling with the subject of instrumental music. What I had failed to remember is that this man considered himself an expert debater on the subject. In past conversations he claimed to have vanquished every opponent who attempted to prove it was permissible to worship God with musical instruments.

The conversation started calmly enough. We reclined in his office sipping coffee. As was his custom, he sat in his black, tall-back tufted leather chair behind a fine oak desk. I sat in the white vinyl chair to the left of the desk. "I've got to be honest with you, Mark," I started, "I am having real misgivings about our church's position on instrumental music." He smiled and asked what was troubling me. I went on to explain that there are problems with the way we arrive at our conclusion that musical instruments in Christian worship are forbidden.

We don't interpret the silence of Scripture consistently, I told him. Take for example the subject of birth control – another matter about which Scripture is silent. Although our denomination has no standard position on the subject, most teachers, I said, traditionally offer advice that goes something like this: "The Bible does not give us any specific instructions about birth control. We are told to be fruitful and multiply, but given the world's booming population, it seems safe to assume that we have fulfilled this mandate. Only once is a form of birth control condemned (see Genesis 38:1–10), but there were extenuating circumstances that do not apply to our day. While we should consider forms of birth control that result in the termination of human life off limits, we have to conclude that Scripture otherwise leaves the matter open ended."

In the case of birth control, I said, we conclude that the silence of Scripture implies that it is permissible. Yet when it comes to instrumental music, we say that the Bible's silence means that it's off limits. The subject matter may be different, I argued, but our interpretive approach should be the same in each instance. If not, why not? Either the silence of Scripture means we that can do something or it means we cannot. We have no basis to insist that it means one thing here and another thing there.

Mark had no response to the birth control argument, but countered with another point, which he thought would satisfy me. Initially I was impressed, but after a few minutes of talking through the logic of his argument I was able to explain why that line of thinking was fatally flawed. He calmly came at the subject from another angle, but that too, I pointed out, was insufficient. After two more exchanges like this, Mark became angry. He sat up in his chair and pointed his right index finger at my nose. "You better watch yourself!" he snapped. "If you keep this up, you're going to end up in a lot of hot water." Shocked by his reaction, I thanked him for his time and retreated to my office.

"What just happened?" I wondered. One minute we're having a friendly conversation; the next we're having an argument. Then I realized that the reason Mark had gotten so angry was the same reason most people having intellectual exchanges lose their cool – he was out of arguments. Unbeknownst to me, Mark had been throwing out his best stuff – the material that he used to confound all those debating adversaries that he had supposedly tangoed with in the past. Pulling rank was the only move he had left. But my probing was an honest quest for knowledge. I genuinely wanted Mark to help me understand why our denomination's unpopular position on instrumental music was correct. But alas, it seemed that our position on the matter was indefensible.

Even more unsettling to my theological world was what I came to realize about my denomination's second distinguishing peculiarity – its emphasis on baptism. This group believes that a person has to be baptized by immersion in order to be saved. But there's more. Members of this denomination maintain that it is necessary for us to know that baptism is a saving act of obedience at the time of our baptism; otherwise it does not count. Put negatively, if we are not baptized in water – with the "correct understanding" of baptism – we are not rightly related to Jesus Christ, even if we claim him as Savior and Lord. Looking at it now, I am embarrassed to say that I not only believed this myself, I also convinced others to embrace this point of view. But as I continued my journey through seminary and witnessed the fruit of the Spirit in the lives of my professors and fellow students, I knew that this view of baptism could not be correct.

I found myself on the horns of a dilemma. My denomination condemned these people as lost. Yet the fruit of the Spirit was just as evident in their lives as it was in mine, if not more so. I struggled to reconcile my experience of God's saving work in their lives with my understanding of Scripture. Try as I might, I could not find anyone who was writing on the subject of baptism that offered a compelling alternative to the interpretation that I had received from my denomination – that is until I came across the work of New Testament theologian Berkeley Mickelsen.

My first exposure to Dr. Mickelsen was through his well-known book, *Interpreting the Bible*, which was required reading in one of my hardest seminary courses – "Biblical Prolegomena."[4] Mickelsen's book was dense, to say the least, but I appreciated the scholarly rigor. He seemed to support a view of baptism that was strikingly similar to my own. This suspicion was confirmed when he came to our campus to teach a course in New Testament theology. I did not take the course myself, but one of the students taking the course informed me that Dr. Mickelsen had befuddled the class one day by saying, "Most of you have no idea what baptism in the New Testament means. What do you suppose the Apostle Peter meant when he said that 'baptism now saves you'" (1 Peter 3:21)? According to this student the class was dumbfounded. I knew then and there that I had to meet with him to discuss this matter.

I phoned Dr. Mickelsen and he graciously agreed to get together with me. He asked if I was conversant with Greek. I told him that I was and he instructed me to bring my Greek New Testament to the meeting. He was both a brilliant and hospitable man. I felt an instant bond with him. It was amazing to discover how many points we agreed on. But as the conversation continued I began to wonder if he had misunderstood the reason for our visit. He spoke at length about the role of confession in salvation. We visited several New Testament passages that spoke of the need to confess our faith in Christ in order to be saved. We read Matthew 10:32 and its parallel, Luke 12:8, in which Jesus says, "Whoever publicly acknowledges me, the Son of Man will also acknowledge before the angels of God." We looked at Romans 10:9–10, where Paul says that "if you confess with your mouth, 'Jesus is Lord,' and believe in your heart that God raised him from the dead, you will be saved. For it is with your heart that you believe and are justified, and it is with your mouth that you confess and are saved." I wondered if he had forgotten why I asked to meet with him.

Then, as though reading my mind, Dr. Mickelsen smiled and said, "I'll bet you're wondering why we've spent so much time looking at these passages on confession." I admitted that I thought he might have missed the point of our meeting. He continued, "I had to lay the necessary groundwork before looking at the key passage on the subject – Acts 2:38." Dr. Mickelsen was right. This passage, more than any other New Testament text, speaks of the crucial role of baptism: "Peter replied, 'Repent and be baptized, every one of you, in the name of Jesus Christ for the forgiveness of your sins. And you will receive the gift of the Holy Spirit.'"

"The problem with many interpreters," said Dr. Mickelsen "is that they think the word 'for' in this passage means 'because of.' But that preposition never means 'because of.'" I was relieved to hear Dr. Mickelsen say this; for it was precisely the problem I was having with the interpreters who tried to diminish the importance of baptism in Acts 2:38. Theologically speaking, I wanted to embrace the traditional "believers-baptism position" – namely, that baptism functions as "an outward sign of an inward faith," and is administered to those whose sins have already been forgiven. But nowhere in the original language of the New Testament could I find an instance in which the word translated "for" should ever be translated "because of."[5] It was affirming to see this distinguished New Testament scholar arrive at the same conclusion. The phrase in this passage, "for the forgiveness of your sins," means precisely what it says, as Dr. Mickelsen confirmed. But what he said next changed everything.

"The key to interpreting this passage," Dr. Mickelsen pointed out, "is not the phrase, 'for the forgiveness of your sins,' but the one before it: "in the name of Jesus Christ." We were sitting at the small round table in his office, each studiously examining the Greek New Testaments in front of us. Then Dr. Mickelsen stopped and looked up at me. Our eyes met. "Chuck," he asked, "what do you suppose this phrase, 'in the name of Jesus Christ,' means?" I thought for a moment and answered as I had been taught. "It means 'by the authority of Jesus Christ,' right?" He grinned childishly, as though he had a secret that he was dying to tell. "Doesn't it strike you as odd," he continued, "that the preposition in this phrase is the word that's typically translated 'on' or 'upon,' not 'in' or 'by'?"[6]

In all honesty I had never noticed this anomaly. "Now that you mention it," I said, "this does seem to be a strange way of putting it. I guess we would literally translate this phrase, 'on the name of Jesus Christ.' But that doesn't make any sense." My not-making-sense comment was a plea for help. Why, I wondered, would the text say, "Repent and be baptized *on the name of Jesus Christ* . . ." Dr. Mickelsen exuded a teacher's joy at having brought yet another would-be initiate to the place of enlightenment. He took hold of the thick tome, which he had placed on the table before our meeting. It bore the title, *A Greek-English Lexicon of the New Testament and Other Early Christian Literature.* He gleefully turned to the page that addressed this particular use of the word and invited me to come next to him so that I could read the entry for myself. "The preposition as it is used in Acts 2:38 is a confessional formula – look!" he said, pointing at the upper left corner of the page. I followed along as he read. The lexicon said that the formulaic phrase, "on the name of something"[7] means "in connection with, or by the use of, i.e. naming, or calling out, or calling upon the name."[8]

It was like replacing the burned-out bulb on a string of Christmas lights. Instantly all the bulbs sprang to life. Every New Testament passage on baptism was illuminated in a way that I had never seen before. At once I realized that the confessional nature of this phrase in Acts 2:38 completely changes the theological meaning: "Peter replied, 'Repent and be baptized, every one of you, *calling on the name of Jesus Christ for the forgiveness of your sins . . .* '" My mind jumped to 1 Peter 3:21 where the Apostle Peter says that what is "saving" about baptism is not "the removal of dirt from the body," that is, not the physical washing that occurs when one is immersed in water, but "the pledge of a good conscience toward God." The word "pledge" in this passage occurs only here in the New Testament. Scholars are not exactly sure how best to translate the term, but one thing is certain: it describes the oral declaration – the confession – that one makes at the time of his or her baptism. I thought of Ananias's invitation to Saul (who would become St. Paul), "And now what are you waiting for? Get up, be baptized and wash your sins away, *calling on his name*" (Acts 22:16).

The "aha!" of the moment was all over my face. Dr. Mickelsen smiled and nodded, "Now you understand why I started our conversation by talking about confession." He composed this sentence as a statement of fact rather than a question. He could see that I got it. He continued, "Baptism in the New Testament is the occasion in which a person makes his or her initial profession of faith. But keep in mind what Paul said about confession in Romans 10, which scholars like George Beasley-Murray see as a baptismal passage."[9] Pointing to Beasley-Murray's book, which he had also placed on the table before our meeting, Dr. Mickelsen went on to explain that what is saving in baptism is the confession that we make *"with the mouth"* (Romans 10:10). He concluded our session with the following advice: "Chuck, we live in a time when there are many conflicting ideas about baptism. But what is important to bear in mind is that despite these differences, we can rest assured that when a person makes the good confession of faith, he or she is rightly related to Jesus Christ, irrespective of how baptism plays into the equation."

The meeting with Dr. Mickelsen was a significant event. It marked the beginning of my exodus from the denomination that had played so vital a role in my spiritual formation after I left the Catholic Church. This new understanding of baptism, along with the realization that my church's view of instrumental music was fatally flawed, forced me into one the most difficult decisions that I have ever made as a follower of Jesus Christ. It took nearly three years from the date of this meeting for it to become clear that I had no choice but to take leave of this denomination. I tried everything to hang on to the relationships that I cherished and that gave me such comfort and security in the Christian life. At first I assumed the role of a prophet. But it soon became apparent that the leaders of my denomination had no desire to entertain the possibility that their cherished views on baptism and instrumental music might be wrong. Instead, they viewed me as suspect. I found myself having to backpedal in order to convince them that I had not strayed from the truth. I felt hopelessly conflicted.

In a last-ditch effort to stay in fellowship with this denomination I started a new church. I hoped that the autonomy afforded by a more independent setting would give me the breathing room I needed to carry on my ministry without getting bogged down in the doctrinal quagmire of baptism and instrumental music. But that was not to be the case. The newly established congregation attracted several of my denomination's stalwart traditionalists who saw this fledgling work as an opportunity to be big fish in a little pond. Add to that the fact that I was receiving financial help from the congregation that I had served for the past seven years, which left me beholden to their theological ideals. In the end, I found myself in just as untenable a position as I was in before I planted the new church. It became clear that I could not continue to receive financial support from well-meaning Christians who rightfully expected me to promote their doctrinal convictions.

I felt lost and alone. In desperation I called a pastor friend who belonged to the denomination with which the seminary that I attended was affiliated. After giving me some much-needed comfort, he recommended that I contact Bill Hoyt, the executive minister of the regional conference. Bill taught several courses that I had taken at seminary and we had actually talked on several occasions about the possibility of my pastoring one of the churches under his oversight. By this time, however, it had been two years since I graduated seminary and I had not spoken to Bill since. My call to him appeared out of the blue to say the least. "Bill," I began, "I know it's been awhile since we last spoke, but Pastor Steve told me to call you." I went on to describe my circumstances and the difficulty that I had trying to serve in a denomination that I was at odds with theologically. I concluded that this is probably typical of most denominations. Bill immediately warmed to the conversation. He said that the culture of some fellowships tends to be more doctrinaire than it is in others. "I haven't changed my feelings about you, Chuck," he assured me. "Two years ago I thought you'd make a great fit with us and I feel the same way today." He said that a couple of churches were looking for a pastor, but could not guarantee that either would be the best match. He promised to do all he could to find the right place for me and ended the call by saying that he would keep in touch.

The next day I told a friend, a fellow pastor in my denomination, that I would soon be leaving my post at the church plant to assume a pastoral position in another fellowship. I confided that this had been a painful and difficult decision to make, but that it came at the end of a long discernment process that was bathed in prayer. I was sure that I was following God's call. My wife, Dianne, believed as much, I said. Although she was not in the same theological predicament as I, she was convinced that God was the author of this move. My friend thanked me for sharing this news and pledged to pray for us throughout the transition period. However, as soon as he hung up the phone me he called three other pastors in the area, informing them that I was about to jump ship. They agreed that I needed to be straightened out. He called me two days later and announced that he and several other colleagues in ministry wanted to have lunch with me to discuss my decision. He said it was for my own good and that he was merely trying to watch out for my best interests.

We had three meetings over the next two months. Each time we met the pastors urged me to reconsider my decision, and each of their urgings came with a corresponding threat – if I remained intent on departing, they would have no choice but to broadcast the news to those who were financing the church plant. Again, I found myself backpedaling to buy time, which left me feeling ashamed of myself for not having the courage simply to step up and tell the truth about my convictions, irrespective of the consequences. At the last of these lunches I crossed paths with Eric, one of the pastors, in the restroom. It was the only time we had spoken one-on-one about the matter. He was far more sympathetic and discerning of my situation than the others. In fact he shared many of my views. As we stood at the sinks washing our hands, Eric turned to me and said, "Chuck, just do it. Don't be afraid. God won't let you down."

They were the words I needed to hear. I had been paralyzed by so many fears – the fear of financial ruin at a time when Dianne was five months pregnant with our youngest son, Nathan; the fear of being judged by the many people who had played such an important role in my growth as a Christian; the fear of exchanging the familiar for the unfamiliar; the fear of failure; the fear that I might be wrong. Eric's words were God's words. In that exchange God himself was telling me that it was okay to draft my letter of resignation and leave that fellowship once and for all. I drove straight home and told Dianne what I had learned that day. "You're a man of prayer," she said. "I trust that you're doing the right thing." I felt alive and emboldened as I drafted the letter. I made multiple copies, individually addressing each one to the elders of the supporting church and to the dozen or so individuals that were funding our ministry. As I dropped the bundle of envelopes in the mailbox I said, "God, it's all in your hands now."

The Sunday after I mailed the letters I announced my resignation to the two-year-old congregation. The news came as no surprise to several leading families in the congregation. Weeks earlier I had met with some of the key members to inform them of my impending departure and to ask them if they would be willing to serve on a steering committee to help guide the church through this transition. To a person they agreed to do so and promised to keep this to themselves until I made my announcement to the whole group. Only one person, however, was privy to the fact that I intended to leave the denomination.

I read my letter aloud to the church. It included the statement that I would be assuming a pastoral position in another denomination. Shock rippled through the crowd. For some of the denominational stalwarts it would have been no different if I had announced that I was becoming an atheist. After the service a lady who was visiting from out of town confronted me, "You know that you're trading the truth of Christ for a lie, don't you? You are going to hell and you're taking your whole family with you." I told her that I understood why she felt that way and assured her that I too believed the same thing at one time. She shook her head in disgust and walked away. Later that week Dianne fielded phone calls from other well-meaning people with the same message. "I can't believe how judgmental people are," she lamented. "In fact," she continued, "I can't believe that we used to be like that!"

Three months passed before I received the call to serve another church. While some of the brightest days of our lives were just around the corner, we couldn't see that at the time. Many people from our old denomination stuck by us and affirmed that we had done the right thing. But the waiting period – with absolutely nothing on the horizon – was excruciating. To be sure, we had much to be thankful for, including the way God provided for us financially. When my Aunt Clare got wind of what we were doing, she wrote out twenty checks, each for $500.00. She told us to cash the checks as needed and live life as usual. "If you aren't in a church by the time these checks run out," she said firmly, "there's more where that came from." That was late September of 1990. A month earlier I had started the doctoral program at Fuller Seminary.

By Thursday, November 15, the money was almost half gone and there were still no ministry positions in sight. On top of that our beloved cat, Smokey, had been missing since Halloween. Before I left for school that morning Dianne

asked me what I thought might have happened to the cat.
In a complete lapse of sensitivity I said, "Satan worshipers
probably nabbed her and sacrificed her to the devil. We
should have never let her out that night." Later that day
I called from school to check in on the family. Dianne had
just read a letter that arrived in the mail that day. It was
from the elders of the congregation that had supported our
church plant. Its tone was cold and scolding. The elders said
that we were making the mistake of our lives and would
surely not succeed in this new endeavor. This disheartening
message was enough to give Dianne second thoughts about
the dark and uncertain path that we had chosen. When I got
home that night, we knelt together on our bedroom floor and
prayed that God would confirm to us in some tangible way
that we were doing the right thing.

The next day brought no relief to Dianne. By late afternoon
she was in agony over the offhanded comment I made the
day before about Smokey and the Satan worshipers. While I
was away at the local library and five-year-old Krystal and
three-year-old Matthew played together in the living room,
Dianne went into the spare bedroom and closed the door
behind her. She poured out her heart to God, holding nothing
back. "Today it's our cat; tomorrow it will be our children,"
she cried. "Jesus, I need to know that we're following your
will and that you haven't forsaken us. The future looks so
bleak. Please tell me that you are going to take care of us
and that you will protect our children from Satan worshipers
and from anyone else who would harm them. I know you
want me to walk by faith and not by sight, but I need proof
that you are with us and that you will protect us." By now
she was sobbing. Tears mingled with mascara streamed down
her face. She prayed on, "If you brought Smokey home, that
would be a sign that you've heard this prayer. But maybe
she's dead . . . and it would be a freak of nature if you
brought her back from the dead. But all things are possible
with you."

She had been in prayer for over an hour when I arrived
home. It was almost 6 p.m. and dark outside. Little Krystal
and Matthew heard me pull into the driveway and ran out to

greet me. Krystal directed me over to the green metal utility box to the right of the driveway and explained that earlier in the day Matthew had fallen off of it and gotten a boo boo. Matthew proudly displayed the Ninja Turtle band-aid on his left knee. Sensing from the bedroom that the children were no longer in the house, Dianne emerged to see where they had gone. The front door was ajar. By now we were trekking single file up the walkway toward the house. Dianne stood at the entry and watched those who were dearest to her march into the house: Krystal, then Matthew, then me, and then Smokey.

When Dianne saw the cat she screamed at the top of her lungs, "SMOKEY!" The children and I were startled to say the least. Here was their mother, my wife, standing in front of us with thick, black streaks down her face, crying hysterically. "Take it easy," I said. "If you keep shouting like that you'll scare the cat away." Between halting, sobbing breaths, Dianne tried to explain, "You don't know what this means. This is a miracle . . . it's God's sign that he is with us and that we are in his will!" She went on to describe in detail the prayerful exchange she had just finished with God. The cat had been gone fifteen days. None of us that night saw her or heard her. Smokey appeared out of the darkness – for Dianne's eyes only – wearing a strange collar and dragging a broken hind leg.

This event stands as a barren tree experience for Dianne and me and our two older children. Even though Krystal and Matthew were very young at the time, they remember, as though it were yesterday, the night that Smokey came home. The event is memorable for reasons beyond the return of a much-loved pet. It stands as a lasting memorial of God's unfailing love and faithfulness. We knew that we could face the months and years to come with confidence; for even though we did not know what the future held, that night God made it unmistakably clear that we were rightly related to the One who holds the future. In that instance, a moment that would require more imagination to construe as coincidence than providence, God drew near to us and communicated a message of relentless tenderness in near-audible fashion: "Carry on my beloved children. I am pleased with you. I will never abandon you."

God delights to give his children aha! moments that reorient us to the truth that he is all around us, hiding in plain sight, the Extraordinary shrouded in the ordinary. Mystics like Brother Lawrence and Mother Teresa stand with other disciples of their kind as a great cloud of witnesses, bidding us to come and die to the self that sees and hears and tastes and smells and feels with mere fleshly perception and come alive to the world that in fact already exists in Christ – *a new creation!*

10. Overthrow of the Mystics

Oh, the depth of the riches of the wisdom and knowledge of God! How unsearchable his judgments, and his paths beyond tracing out! Who has known the mind of the Lord? Or who has been his counselor? Who has ever given to God, that God should repay him? For from him and through him and to him are all things. To him be the glory forever! Amen.

Romans 11:33–36

We must beware lest we violate the holy, lest our dogmas overtake the mystery.

Abraham Heschel, *I Asked for Wonder*

The Risk of Mystery

Talk of "mystery" and "mystics" makes some modernist Christians very nervous. "Christian mystic" for these people is an oxymoron. They think of mystics as misfits – wild-eyed eccentrics who were considered godly by a church that had already lost its own way. They cite the strange antics of several well-known saints and conclude that no self-respecting disciple in his or her right (modern!) mind could accept such behavior as laudable or godly. St. Francis of Assisi, they surmise, should have been institutionalized – if not for carrying on conversations with "Brother Rabbit" and "Sister Cricket," then for cutting himself and calling it stigmata. (That one could be so mystically identified with the Passion as to manifest the physical characteristics of

Jesus' wounds in his own body starkly violates modern sensibilities.) These modern skeptics would say that St. John, with all his talk of the "dark night of the soul," would have been a good candidate for Prozac or lithium. And all the fasting that St. Catherine of Siena did would qualify her as an anorexic. They suppose that these so called mystics would have fared quite poorly on a modern psychological test like the Minnesota Multiphasic Personality Inventory (MMPI). But when it comes to identifying the unique characteristics of the "people of God" as described in Scripture, our categories for "normal" are inevitably challenged.

Contemporary Western culture domesticates us. There is little if any tolerance for people who tread beyond the bounds of socially acceptable behavior by modern standards. When we encounter people who do, even if they do so to the glory of God, our first instinct is to consider them a nuisance. Bob comes to mind. He used to attend the Bible study that Dianne and I conducted on the grass at Mesa College in San Diego. Several college-age members of our church attended Mesa at the time. They talked us into visiting the campus every Wednesday afternoon to hold an informal question-and-answer session with interested students. Bob was among them.

Looking back on it now, I can see that Bob was a mystic. At the time, however, most of us in the group didn't know what to make of him. His questions and comments routinely came out of left field. It was like he was tuned to a different channel. He would stop halfway into a sentence, look off into space, and laugh as though he were in conversation with an unseen visitor. "Oh, that's good," he would say with a trance-like look on his face, "I hadn't thought of it that way before . . . thank you, Jesus." He said that he was conscious of Jesus' presence every waking moment. He routinely consulted Jesus on what clothes to wear that day, when to go to the bathroom, what to eat for lunch, and whether he should answer the phone when it rang. By all other accounts, Bob was a fully functioning human being. He was intelligent, socially adept, successful in business, and an exemplary student. And on top of that, he possessed an extraordinary apprehension of things spiritual. I suspect that he and Brother Lawrence would have gotten along famously.

Spiritual experiences do not need to be strange or out of place to qualify as "mystical." Theologian Carole Spencer, my colleague and resident expert on mystics at George Fox Evangelical Seminary, says that being open to mystery "doesn't necessarily mean that one becomes a total space cadet." She continues:

> I believe that most genuine mystics are known only to God, and are not necessarily odd to most people, nor would they be immediately labeled as mystics. I know a number of people I would call mystics, who are quite rational and function normally in most arenas, though quite often they are prophetic individuals who challenge and critique the Christian status quo.[1]

And the contemporary church stands in urgent need of more prophetic individuals.

While the pursuit of mystery may seem irrelevant and ill-advised to our modernist counterparts in the faith, the risk of not doing so is evident by where we've ended up after 400 years of enlightened Christianity. With the exception of Quakerism, Pentecostalism, and the Protestant and Roman Catholic charismatic renewal movements, Christian spirituality in the West has been largely subdued by the way of knowledge and the way of piety. Christians over the past several centuries pursued knowledge and personal piety as the primary means of spiritual growth while matters of faith were simultaneously sterilized of mystery. Historians like Louis Cognet reflect upon this as "the overthrow of the mystics."[2] But the downfall of mystery didn't happen overnight.

The Flight from Mystery

The retreat from Christianity's mystical impulses can be traced all the way back to St. Augustine (353–430). His work marks the dividing line in the history of Western thought between the classical world of the Roman Empire and the Middle Ages. Augustine was actually as much a mystic as an intellectual. But his scholarly work proved more enduring, earning him a seat in Christian history as the church's greatest early theologian. Augustine's intellectualism also set in motion the drift toward scholasticism, which culminated in the formation of the university some 800 years later.

Twelfth-century Augustinian thinkers like Anselm and Peter Abelard tried to preserve the balance between matters of the mind and Spirit by describing Christian spirituality as "faith seeking understanding" and demonstrating the coherence between revealed truth and rational truth. But by the thirteenth century the already-strained rift between mysticism and scholasticism reached the breaking point when theological reflection finally moved out of the churches and monasteries and into the newly established university. Thomas Aquinas' pronouncement in the thirteenth century that theology is "the Queen of the sciences" marks the decisive point at which the peaceful coexistence between the Church's mystical and scholastic traditions met its end.

From the time of the apostles to the beginning of the Renaissance, mystics were just as influential as intellectuals in the formation of the church's theology and spirituality. Perhaps the most notable case in point is Dionysius the Areopagite, a late-fifth- or early sixth-century mystic and theologian whose writings impacted the Western and Eastern church for more than ten centuries. We know nothing about the man himself other than what we can gather from his written work. He identified himself with the Dionysius who was converted by the Apostle Paul (see Acts 17:34), yet the writings themselves reflect the influence of Proclus, the great fifth-century sage of the Platonic school in Athens. He was most likely either a pupil of Proclus himself or one his early sixth-century successors. His written work was probably completed somewhere between AD 485 and 528.

Many modern scholars claim that Dionysius' self-identification with the first-century figure by the same name qualifies him as a deceiver. They've named him Pseudo-Dionysius and consider his work a forgery. However, as

Kevin Corrigan and Michael Harrington correctly point out, "forgery" is a modern notion: "Adopting the persona of an ancient figure was a long established rhetorical device (known as *declamatio*), and others in Dionysius' circle also adopted pseudonymous names from the New Testament." They argue that it is a mistake to consider Dionysius' works a forgery in the modern sense. Rather, Dionysius identifies himself with the first-century Areopagite as "an acknowledgement of reception and transmission, namely, a kind of coded recognition that the resonances of any sacred undertaking are intertextual, bringing the diachronic structures of time and space together in a synchronic way, and that this theological teaching, at least, is dialectically received from another."[3] In other words, Dionysius felt a special affinity with this New Testament figure. In assuming his name, he was attempting to put himself into his first-century compatriot's sandals – to see the world as he saw it, and to give expression to his own thoughts accordingly. To accuse him of trying to deceive his readers, therefore, is to illegitimately read modern literary standards back into another time and culture.

From the sixth to the sixteenth century, Dionysius consistently made the Who's Who of the most influential people from both mystical and intellectual traditions. He is quoted by the likes of Eulogius, Patriarch of Alexandria and Pope Gregory the Great. He is appealed to by the architects of the Lateran Council, Pope Martin I, Pope Agatho, the Sixth Ecumenical Council of Constantinople, and the second Council of Nicaea. The Byzantine Emperor, Michael, gifted a copy of Dionysius' writings to Louis I of France. John Scotus translated his work into Latin. The papal librarian, Anastasius, commented on his writings. Medieval scholastics like Peter Lombard, Alexander of Hales, Albertus Magnus, and Bonaventure held his work in high esteem, adopting many of his ideas and arguments. High-profile personalities of mystical and intellectual perspectives wrote commentaries on his work, including the mystic, Hugh of St. Victor, and one of the greatest intellectuals of the church, Thomas Aquinas. Aquinas' greatest theological works, in fact, are said to house – like honey in a beehive – the best of Dionysius' thought.[4]

In classic mystical fashion, Dionysius claimed that we cannot experience a full encounter with God until we abandon all efforts to achieve it by means of our own knowledge or effort. In his well-known treatise, *Mystical Theology*, he spoke of Moses' encounter with God, saying that "he did not attain to the Presence of God itself; he did not see it (for it cannot be looked upon) . . ." The most we can see with our eyes or comprehend with our minds are "symbolical expressions" of ultimate reality. But, said Dionysius, this "incomprehensible Presence" will break forth when we leave behind the senses and the operations of the intellect and reach toward the "unknowing" that transcends all being and all knowledge. This in turn

> plunges the mystic into the Darkness of Unknowing, whence all perfection of understanding is excluded, and he is enwrapped in that which is altogether intangible, wholly absorbed in what is beyond all, and in none else (whether himself or another); and through the inactivity of all his reasoning powers is united by his highest faculty to what is wholly unknowable; thus by knowing nothing he knows That which is beyond his knowledge.[5]

Dionysius' influence notwithstanding, when Aquinas crowned theology the queen of the sciences, he set it squarely in the domain of the university, separating theological reflection from the church and from its much-needed mystical component. And with the emergence of Protestantism in the early sixteenth century, and the violence that followed in the seventeenth century, the pursuit of mystery was the last thing on people's minds.

The Problem of Many Authorities

The Western church's growing distaste for mystery has much to do with the so-called "problem of many authorities," a term coined by Princeton University historian, Jeffrey Stout. The quest to experience the immediacy of God's presence was suppressed by the more urgent need to regain a sense of certainty and order at a time when established authorities were no longer speaking with one voice and it was "anything but clear which opinions one should accept."[6] Protestant spirituality became more uniformly rational and materialistic as it allied itself with the mainstream of Enlightenment thought, which was driven by the quest for a "neutral authority" that could be justified by human reason. The goal, as we observed earlier, was to identify the firm foundation upon which all human knowledge is based, and on which all could agree.

The Catholic Church remained more tolerant of mystics than Protestants, so long as they didn't rock the boat by questioning the legitimacy of the institutional Church. Still, with a few notable exceptions, mysticism in both mainstream Catholic and Protestant camps was confined to the edges until the latter half of the twentieth century. At that point Pentecostal spirituality became more widespread as charismatic renewal movements swept through many Catholic and Protestant congregations. The mysticism of Ignatius of Loyola, which emphasizes discernment and spiritual direction, became more popular among an influential minority of Roman Catholics and Protestants. The works of John of the Cross, Teresa of Avila, Brother Lawrence, and twentieth-century Catholic contemplative, Thomas Merton, also enjoyed unprecedented popularity. Ironically, however, even though there was a fair share of Christian mystics outside Roman Catholicism – such as Jakob Boehme and George Fox – many Protestants today, from both fundamentalist and liberal camps, maintain that so-called Christian mysticism is essentially a Catholic phenomenon with non-Christian roots.[7]

Faithfulness versus Perfection

Honest followers of Christ – Catholics and Protestants alike – will question whether we have ever been at our best as God's people. The reflection on Christian life and thought from the time of the apostles to the present is, in a word, the study of *our struggle* – the struggle of imperfect disciples who are trying to find their way amid a host of competing social and, dare we say, demonic influences. The outcomes of this struggle have always been mixed. In each generation we have gotten some things absolutely right while at the same time overlooking and, in some cases, trampling upon other important truths and practices. Our struggle has never been without its flaws and failures. Happily, by God's grace, our faithfulness to his way is not measured by human perfection. In fact God has already factored our imperfection into the equation (see Romans 8).

The findings and formulations of the twenty-one ecumenical councils of the Roman Catholic Church, from the First Council of Nicaea to the Second Vatican Council, reflect our best Western-Catholic efforts to be faithful to the way of Christ in each generation. Would we do some things differently and undo other things completely if we had the chance to repeat history? Most of us would say "yes." Such matters are always much clearer in hindsight. Would Luther edit some of his sermons or modify his lurid cartoons depicting the pope and other Catholic magistrates if he were given the opportunity to do so? Hopefully. Would Calvin write his theology the same way today? Probably not.

The experience that Thomas Aquinas had at the end of his life comes to mind. Remember that the Catholic Church canonized Thomas as a saint because it believed his theological wisdom was of supernatural origin. But as he was nearing completion of his magnum opus, his *Summa Theologica*, he had a mystical experience that stopped him in his tracks. It happened while he was worshiping at mass on December 6, 1273. All at once the veil was lifted and he saw the things of God as never before – *a new creation!* experience. Afterwards he said, "All that I have written seems to me like straw compared to what has now been revealed to me." At that, Thomas set down his quill, never to write another word of theology. A brief encounter with mystery was enough to displace a lifetime of studious theological reflection.

The point is that as long as we live on this side of glory we will never follow God's way perfectly. This is why it is so important for our faith communities to provide safe places for us to take off our masks and draw strength from each other while in the troughs of our undulating spirituality. Scripture again and again attests to the irreplaceable value of *togetherness* in the formation of our souls (see, for example, Hebrews 3:12, 13). It is in the context of *church* (our gathered selves) that we rejoice with those who rejoice and weep with those who weep (Romans 12:15). Together we bear one another's burdens and gently rescue those of our fold who are caught in sin – humbly acknowledging that we too are no less subject to temptation (Galatians 6:1, 2). Together we engage in the powerful practice of corporate spiritual discernment by which we hear and follow the voice of our present Lord. And through this process, we discover precisely how our Lord has called us and gifted us to live out our salvation in the here and now (Romans 12:3–13).

Spiritual Archaeology

The foregoing, of course, is an idealized portrayal of the church. We must resist the temptation to hold ourselves to a standard that we will seldom if ever achieve. Some disciples think that we need to restore the church to its original, first-century form. Only then, they say, will we have the "true church" that Christ intended. But such wishful thinking begs the question, which first-century church? It took divine intervention and outright persecution to get the Jerusalem church to expand its witness to Samaria and beyond, and in the absence of any sustained evangelistic activity, the bulk of the early church's missionary enterprise eventually fell to the church of Antioch. The church of Thessalonica needed to be encouraged to excel more and more and not succumb to spiritual anemia. The Galatian churches were, in the words of St. Paul, in danger of falling from grace. The Corinthian Christians were plagued with a variety of maladies, including divisions, sexual immorality, and spiritual elitism. The church at Colossae was flirting with false teaching and the church at Rome was conflicted over questions about what sort of behavior constitutes "weaker" and "stronger" Christians. It is worth noting that when Jesus addressed the seven churches of Asia Minor in the opening chapters of Revelation, only two of the five got off without being cited for some spiritual infraction (or worse). If that is any indication of our present state, we might expect Jesus to have similar criticisms of about 70 percent of today's churches. There's never been the perfect church, if by "perfect" we mean theological and behavioral perfection.

The New Testament does not give us a model church to replicate in our day in order to be faithful. It gives us the same testimony that the rest of church history gives us – that of imperfect people, just like you and me, trying to sort out how best to follow the way of Christ in their time and place. Getting this fact into our heads and hearts should be enough to rouse us from idealistic notions that make us think of Pentecost as the perfect beginning to which we must return rather than the church's Big Bang that impels us away from itself and into the future. We do not become faithful followers of Jesus by returning to some point in the past. We are most faithful when we are present to Jesus' presence and obedient to his leading. We do not study Scripture and church history in order to *go back*. Rather, as Mennonite theologian John Howard Yoder put it, we do so in order to *"loop back"* and recover from the past whatever we left behind, "whose pertinence was not seen before."[8]

Spiritual Discernment – Theology of the People

My claim in this chapter is that we have been so distracted by post-Enlightenment modes of thinking that we haven't even noticed what's missing in our spirituality. Most of us are strangers to mystery. Theological reflection is the practice of academicians, not that of average, everyday disciples. Church is a thing of our own making and exists, if we choose to avail ourselves of its goods and services, for our own personal benefit.

If St. Paul were to visit some of our fine churches today, it's a safe bet he would be ramping up his epistle-writing ministry again. Perhaps he would use blogs and emails this time around. What's important to note is that Paul produced his greatest theological works for churches, not for theologians. In fact most of the New Testament was written to local congregations. While some in the early church were more educated than others, there was no such thing as a guild of scholars that did the church's thinking on its behalf. Theological reflection was mainly the practice of local gatherings of disciples that came together with the realization that Christ also was in their midst. They read Scripture and prayed. They fasted and worshiped. They heard and obeyed the voice of the Holy Spirit (see Acts 13:1–3). Those who participated in the Jerusalem Council followed the same pattern, so that in the end they could say, "It seemed good to the Holy Spirit and to us . . ." (Acts 15:28). Theological reflection, in other words, was *spiritual discernment* in which disciples engaged the wondrous mystery of Christ's presence more than their own intellects.

Spiritual discernment – church-based theological reflection that engages the mystery of Christ's presence – is exactly what we've been missing for the last 400 years. While mystery was shoved to the sidelines and theological reflection was carried on in ivory towers, we were left to our own devices to sort out how best to be disciples of Jesus. Not surprisingly we made some mistakes. But rising above these mistakes is accomplished by going forward, not backward. To be sure, we must "loop back" and recover mystery, but then we must face forward and take our stand on the shoulders of our faithful predecessors, both recent and ancient. The way of mystery cannot be isolated from the way of knowledge and the way of piety, for they too are a valuable part of our history. As the way of mystery draws on both the resources of our minds and our bodies, from both right belief and right behavior, it is actually helped by its two more recent counterparts. All three ways in fact have their origins in Scripture, which we will consider shortly. In the next chapter, however, we glance over the shoulder at our most recent, modern past in hopes of discerning our present state more clearly.

11. Christianity à la Carte

Since, then, you have been raised with Christ, set your hearts on things above, where Christ is seated at the right hand of God. Set your minds on things above, not on earthly things. For you died, and your life is now hidden with Christ in God.

Colossians 3:1–3

The more we focus on ourselves, the smaller our world becomes. But if we turn our eyes upward from the dusty paths of this world to the glory of heaven, our world becomes bigger, richer, and filled with glory we never imagined.

Kevin G. Harney, *Seismic Shifts*

Soul Dissonance

Dallas Willard makes the stunning-but-true observation that human beings can honestly profess to believe what they do not in fact believe. "They may do this for so long," says Willard, "that even they no longer know that they do not believe what they profess." Their actions, of course, are consistent with what they actually believe. The problem is that they don't know what they actually believe. The outcome of this dissonance between profession and practice is that "they will lose themselves in bewilderment about the weakness of their 'faith.'" Most astonishing of all is that this is not only a problem for humans in general. "That bewilderment," says Willard, "is a common condition among professing Christians today." Quoting a well-known management principle, Willard offers this hard-hitting explanation: "Your system is perfectly designed to produce the result you are getting."[1]

Why do so many Christians struggle spiritually? Willard's allusion to "system" is our cue. Relational systems experts, Michael C. Armour and Don Browning, point out that human community "always reflects the distinctive influence of the prevailing dominant system among the group's members. This is true whether we are speaking of institutions, organizations, congregations, or even entire civilizations."[2] They distinguish between "casual models" and "core models." We tend to hold casual models lightly and replace them quickly when new information comes along that challenges us to change our thinking or behavior. For example, my wife Dianne for years taught "Step," a very popular form of aerobic exercise. She loves it. But when we moved to Oregon and she took a position at the local YMCA, she was required to teach floor aerobics, which is not as popular. Even though Dianne prefers to teach Step, she made the transition effortlessly. Her association with Step and fellow Step instructors is, in Armour and Browning's terms, "a casual model."

Core models are different. They embody the very essence of who we are and therefore are anything but casual. Local congregations are core models – communal systems that embrace our most deeply held beliefs about ourselves and the ultimate meaning of life. The problem is that our church-based core systems are often flawed. This occurs when they absorb ideals and assumptions from the wider culture that clash with the norms of Scripture. When this happens, what we claim to believe as a group differs from what we actually believe. All the while our lives are directed by an elusive set of hidden beliefs. It becomes almost impossible to sort out what it means to be "a faithful Christian."

There are reasons for this disconnect between professed belief and actual belief. We are the products of a conflicted age. We inhabit the secular world and the sacred world – the sphere of commonly held cultural norms and the sphere of personally held beliefs. When I was seven years old my friend announced that his parents were Republicans. He asked if

my parents were too. I thought so, but I told him I'd make
sure. That night I asked my mother if she was Republican.
She said absolutely not and wondered why I had thought
such an awful thing. I told her about the conversation with
my friend and she proceeded to give me a lesson about the
difference between public discourse and private discourse.
"There are two things we never talk about in public," she
stressed, "religion and politics." I was shocked. "Things we
can't talk about? How strange."

Mental health experts describe the devastating effects of
"cognitive dissonance" – a phenomenon that occurs when we
hold conflicting beliefs and attitudes simultaneously. When
we embrace Jesus as Lord of all things, seen and unseen,
and then try to live by the conflicting rules of two worlds,
we set ourselves up for another deadly form of dissonance
– *soul dissonance*. Soul dissonance occurs when we try to live
as functional secularists in the public domain and followers
of Christ in the private domain. We are neither our best as
citizens of the world or as disciples of Jesus Christ.

The story of how we came to experience the world in two
parts is complicated. We have a good many lawyer jokes at
our disposal, but much the same humor can be applied to
philosophers. The many variations of the well-known how-
many-people-does-it-take-to-screw-in-a-light-bulb theme are
surely more inspired by philosophy than jurisprudence. Much
of our thinking about ourselves and the world is influenced
by modern philosophers like Francis Bacon, René Descartes,
John Locke, David Hume, Immanuel Kant, and Thomas Reid.
This isn't new.

Christians in the West have a long tradition of drawing from
great philosophers. Augustine in the fifth century relied on
Plato. Aquinas in the thirteenth century drew from Aristotle.
Schleiermacher in the nineteenth century presupposed Kant.
Likewise, theologians Charles Hodge and B. B. Warfield
in the nineteenth century were indebted to Francis Bacon
and Thomas Reid. Twentieth-century theologian Karl Barth
borrowed heavily from both Hegel and Kant. In short, if we
want to blame anybody today for our two-part world, we can
blame modern philosophers and those who followed them.

We should note, of course, that Christianity has never existed in an a-cultural vacuum. Culture, if you will, is like the container into which the life-giving water of Christ is poured, assuming its shape and filling it with new meaning. The story of Israel and Jesus must always converge with our story if there is to be any meaningful engagement with truth at all. But there is always the risk that culture may in some way dilute this water, rendering it poisonous and undrinkable. Yale University historian, Roland H. Bainton, frames our challenge as well as anyone. He said, ". . . if there is no accommodation, Christianity is unintelligible and cannot spread. If there is too much accommodation it will spread, but will no longer be Christianity."[3]

If there is any point at which we have teetered too closely to the brink of over-accommodation, it is on the subject of what sociologist Robert N. Bellah and others call, "ontological individualism."[4] Philosophers like John Locke believed that human beings exist first and foremost as individuals and that affiliation with any form of community is strictly voluntary – and secondary to our existence as human beings. They believed that human rationality was unaffected by our social contexts. The pursuit of truth was seen as the work of solitary individuals who were engaged in pure research apart from the social structures around them.

Locke then applied what he thought about human existence to the church, offering the following description that many modern Christians eventually adopted as gospel:

> Let us now consider what a church is. A church, then, I take to be a voluntary society of men, joining themselves together of their own accord in order to the public worshipping of God, in such manner as they judge acceptable to Him, and effectual to the salvation of their souls.[5]

This virulent strain of individualism became the basis on which philosophers like Immanuel Kant would drive a wedge into our world, sundering it in two. But even more devastating is the way it redefined the church. Rather than seeing the church as something of God's making, which he conceived before the creation of the world, many Christians in the modern world have come to see it as a thing of human making – fashioned by our "own accord" and in a manner that we judge acceptable. Eventually the growing affluence that accompanied industrialization combined with this ideology of individualism, spawning a force that profoundly shaped the modern Western world and beyond namely, consumerism.[6]

The Have-it-your-way Church

With the bulk of theological reflection being carried on in universities and mystical experiences of Jesus' presence relegated to the sidelines, the Western church throughout the last 400 years suffered an identity crisis in which it saw itself as an ad hoc collection of individuals gathered, in the spirit of enlightened self-interest, for mutually edifying public worship and for the obtaining of personal salvation. This understanding of the church's nature altered the way we envisioned pastoral leadership and the role of the laity.

Pastor's new job description

The modern pastor's "job description" was defined along the lines of three roles whose aim was to foster a user-friendly environment for church members: the pastor as *therapist*, the pastor as *teacher*, and the pastor as *CEO*. Each emphasis reflects a loss of pastoral identity.[7]

Pastor-as-therapist. To combine the roles of pastor and therapist is to create a new profession that bears little resemblance to historical pastoral identity.[8] The main occupation of the pastor-as-therapist is to provide help and healing to needy souls.

One of my predecessors was a pastor-therapist. When I began my service as senior pastor of that particular church, I discovered to my dismay that I had inherited an entirely different set of expectations than I was used to. Both the staff and the parishioners believed that the pastor should be consumed with care giving. They did not consider me a true shepherd unless I took the initiative to spend *all* my time with the flock. It was my job to seek out and bring healing to every hurting soul. On one occasion I had to drive one of our aged members to the hospital while he appeared to be having a heart attack. It was a given that this was the pastor's job. But I was trained under the "pastor-as-teacher" model, which also has its drawbacks.

Pastor-as-teacher. As the "way of knowledge" gained acceptance as a route to spiritual maturity, preaching in the modern church took on new significance, and the pastor became the prophetic educator of the local church. In many Protestant traditions the sermon is viewed as the crowning event of the worship service. The effectiveness of congregational singing, corporate prayer, the offering of gifts, and even the Eucharist is measured in terms of "how well they prepare the parishioners' hearts and minds for sermon."

Many modern church attendees, for their part, choose to join a given congregation on the basis of whether they are "fed" (they would never use the word, "entertained") by the preaching. This condition has led to a blurring of pastoral identity. Wes Roberts and Glenn Marshall observe that church for most people means "getting together for worship." The Sunday service is a production and the success or failure of this production is assessed on the basis of "how the preacher performs in the pulpit."[9]

Pastor-as-CEO. The most talented preachers have gained huge followings that require large support staffs, sprawling facilities, and multimillion-dollar budgets. The challenges associated with such ministries have driven a growing number of these pastors to seek out the leadership skills necessary to make them equal to the task. And those who want to reap the same fruits as their megachurch counterparts often seek to do so by means of similar leadership methods. The last quarter of the twentieth century witnessed more books written for pastors on "leadership" than on all other aspects of pastoral ministry combined.[10] The pastor as CEO was born and, as Ben Patterson points out tongue-in-cheek, the professionalization of clergy along the lines of the secular business model has produced yet another identity crisis for the pastor: "Well-dressed and well-spoken, armed with degrees, leadership savvy, management manuals, and marketing studies – all to be used for the good of the kingdom, of course – we intend to make a mark on the world, gain a little respect for the profession, and shed forever the pastor's Rodney Dangerfield image."[11]

All in all, good pastors in the modern church are distinguished from not-so-good pastors by their ability to care well, preach well, and lead well. This view of pastoral ministry not only defined the criteria for pastoral success. It also worked to keep pastors so preoccupied with "ministry" (variously defined) that they had little time for the more biblically pastoral work of leading the church in the discernment, development, and deployment of its manifold spiritual gifts.

Church Driven by the *Wrong* Purpose

Just as Locke's individualism inspired us to see the church as a voluntary society of individuals, the spirit of consumerism was equally influential in defining the church's purpose in the world. This is where we see the real rub between our professed beliefs and our actual beliefs. If we were to ask, "Why does the church exist?" most Christians could offer reasonably sound theological responses: "The church exists to worship and glorify God"; "The church exists to make disciples"; or "The church exists to further God's mission in the world." Such *professions* regarding the church's purpose are correct, to be sure. But what we *actually believe* about the church's purpose is reflected in how we *do church*. It will help our cause, therefore, to reflect briefly on how the influences of consumerism have redefined the church's purpose. We will consider three areas of the Christian life that typically serve as focal points of the church's purpose: worship, discipleship, and witness.

Worship

Modern Protestant Christians have tended to think of gathered worship along the lines of two main goals – one pertaining to believers and the other to nonbelievers. With regard to believers the goal of the service is to strengthen our faith by imparting godly knowledge and urging us to live godly lives. The main goal pertaining to unbelievers is evangelism. This second focus came into play as the result of revivalism, which first appeared in the eighteenth century and became a potent force in the nineteenth and twentieth centuries.

Revivalism brought about widespread spiritual awakenings that changed our entire perspective on gathered worship. Up until the eighteenth century, corporate Christian worship adhered for the most part to the liturgical patterns that were first adapted from the synagogue in the first and second centuries. Such common expressions as "Amen," "Alleluia," "Lord have mercy," "Thanks be to God," "Forever and ever," and "Blessed are you, O Lord our God" all came from the liturgy of the synagogue. In the late fourth and early fifth centuries the liturgy was standardized in the form of the "Roman Rite" under the initiative of Pope Damasus I. In the Protestant Reformation movement the center of the liturgy shifted from the Eucharist to the preached word, but gathered worship continued to follow the basic format of the Roman Rite. With few exceptions worship retained this liturgical structure until the eighteenth century.

Between 1730 and 1745 revival swept across the American colonies. Puritan theologian Jonathan Edwards referred to this as the "surprising work of God," but it was remembered by later generations as the Great Awakening. The onset of the Revolutionary War brought an end to revival in most quarters. One notable exception, however, was the Methodists, who did not arrive in North America until 1766. During the war, revivalism continued as a vital influence within Methodist circles, both shaping and being shaped by Wesleyan-Arminian thought.

In the nineteenth century, revivalism reemerged in the Christian mainstream, but this time with much greater emphasis on the role of the individual's freedom to choose. Evangelistic tent meetings became widespread, reshaping the landscape of American Christianity. By the mid nineteenth century, a growing number of churches had either come into existence or experienced spiritual renewal through revivals. As a result, their worship services were modeled less after historic liturgies and more after evangelistic tent meetings. From the late nineteenth century on, many American churches considered the worship service to be the primary vehicle of evangelism.[12]

Twentieth-century Catholic Christians witnessed many sweeping changes in their gathered worship as well. The Constitution on the Sacred Liturgy of the Second Vatican Council (1962–5) substantially revised the Mass. The Mass was now to be held in the native languages of the people rather than in Latin. Congregational singing was emphasized as never before. Additional eucharistic prayers were added and the laity was allowed to partake of both the bread and wine (previously lay persons were allowed only to partake of the bread). And priests celebrated the Mass facing the gathered worshipers rather than the front of the sanctuary, with their backs to the people.

These last two alterations are most significant in that they mark a substantial increase in the importance placed on the laity in worship and a shifting of the priest's function – from sole mediator to the one who presides over *gathered* eucharistic worship. Before Vatican II, the church considered it sufficient for priests alone to partake of the eucharistic wine – they did so for all the people. Priests celebrated the Mass with their backs to the congregation – and could do so without anyone present at all. The priest was our mediator, the Mass's lone celebrant on behalf of the many absent. His worship was our worship. The laity's showing up was optional. With the changes enacted by Vatican II, however, the priest is no longer permitted to celebrate the Mass if no one shows up. The priest's role in Mass is one of *facilitator of gathered worship*. It falls to the people of God to assemble and partake of Eucharist together, in its complete form (bread *and* wine). The people matter: no worshipers, no worship.

This shift triggered a corresponding response on the part of the Catholic Church: *entice more worshipers to come.* Forward-thinking bishops authorized changes in the Mass that promised to draw more of the faithful back to church, especially from the younger generation. The "Folk Mass" was introduced, which brought drums, electric guitars, and colorfully clad vocalists and musicians to the front of the sanctuary – sharing sacred space with the altar and lecterns.

I will never forget the first Folk Mass that my family and I attended at my home church, St. Brigid Catholic Church. For me, it was a breath of fresh air. I loved it. So far as my parents were concerned, however, it was a disaster. They hated it. They were appalled that "hippies with their disrespectful dress and profane instruments would be allowed to put on such a display at church – and right next to the altar no less!" For the first time, Catholics were introduced to what had, up to that point, been a predominantly Protestant phenomenon – *worship wars*. While the changes inaugurated by Vatican II were much needed and most helpful in revitalizing Roman Catholicism, they unwittingly opened the Catholic Church to the same sort of consumerist appetites that induce many Protestants to come to church.

All in all, the church in the twentieth century experienced unprecedented numerical growth. But the aim of gathered worship was often (unknowingly) shaped by the ideals of consumerism: *promise to meet their needs and they will come; meet their needs and they will stay.* We look now to "the group that stays" as we consider the impact of consumerism on the modern church's approach to discipleship.

Discipleship

When the church draws people into its orbit by means of the gravitational pull of self-interest, we shouldn't be surprised when such persons assume the posture of religious consumers. The goods to be consumed include personal salvation, mutually satisfying social experiences, and uplifting worship services.

The religious consumer sees him- or herself as a self-directed individual. For one to become a "disciple" in the biblical sense requires a paradigm shift in the way we understand the nature of personhood. By biblical definition a disciple is one who has relinquished the privileges and prerogatives of autonomous selfhood to become the loyal follower of another. But modern individualism has taught us to believe that we are thinking selves in the first order. While we may benefit from the ideas and insights of others, it remains for *us* to decide which ideas and insights to accept or reject. "After all," says modern individualism, "we can't follow any teacher unconditionally, for the problem of many authorities is still around." Of course these notions of individualism highlight an essential truth about ourselves: *we think the way we do because our world – including the church – has trained us to think that way.*

According to the canons of individualistic consumerism, the choice to align ourselves with a local church is seen as optional to faithful discipleship. We can have a personal relationship with Jesus Christ and follow him faithfully without ever getting involved with other believers. Discipleship is defined by the acquisition of spiritual knowledge and the exercise of Christian virtues – both of which can be achieved by the solitary individual. This of course is to construe discipleship in a way that Scripture never envisions. To early Christians it would have been inconceivable for one to choose Christ but not the local church. Consumerist notions of discipleship have also had an impact on our function as Christ's witnesses in the world.

Witness

By the beginning of the twentieth century the modern church in North America came to conceive of the church's witness in two distinct modes. "Liberals" resonated with the mode of witness popularized by Walter Rauschenbusch (1861–1918), the celebrated originator of the Social Gospel. Son of German immigrant parents, Rauschenbusch began his first pastorate in Manhattan where he encountered the devastating injustices of urban life. Though deeply influenced by the individualism of his conversion, he came to realize that the church must not only emphasize personal salvation; it must also seek to bring about the transformation of social structures.[13] His views exerted an abiding influence on liberal Protestant churches throughout the better part of the twentieth century, even though the Social Gospel movement as such lost much of its appeal after the rise of the organized labor movement in the early twentieth century. As time went on, social action in many liberal Protestant circles eclipsed personal conversation as the primary vehicle of Christ's witness to the world. To care for the needy and defend the cause of the downtrodden is considered adequate enough fulfillment of Christ's mission in the world. The goal of our witness for liberal Christians, in other words, is the eradication of sin in the form of social injustice.

"Conservatives," on the other hand, emphasized the need for personal conversion. As was noted above, revivalism exerted a strong influence on the shaping of Christianity in North America in the nineteenth and twentieth centuries. Second-wave revival began in the early nineteenth century and was rooted in the Wesleyan-Arminian theological tradition. Rather than stressing God's sovereignty in the role of salvation, as revivals of the Great Awakening did a century earlier, nineteenth- and twentieth-century revivalism was much more congenial to the spirit of democracy that had taken hold of the nation.[14] One principal distinctive of second-wave revival is the emphasis it placed on "unlimited atonement," which underscores the conviction that the benefits and blessings of Christ's sacrifice are available to all who choose them.[15] By the end of the nineteenth century the evangelistic practices of most churches were steeped in Arminian thought – even though most people knew little if anything of Arminius himself. And the influence of Arminianism has persisted, as historian Alistair Mason observes: "The majority of Christians would like to think that Christ died for all. Few people have ever read Arminius, or reworked the classic debates, but the unconsidered assumptions of most Protestants are now Arminian."[16] Second-wave revivalism therefore has not only shaped the way evangelical Christians worship; it also influences the way they evangelize.

Conclusion

Without the much-needed service of spiritual discernment, the church in the modern period was left without the higher-order reflection needed to test its practices in the light of both Scripture and the guidance of Christ's present leadership. In the absence of this essential discernment element the followers of Christ have suffered from "soul dissonance" with regard to its nature and purpose.

The church's *nature* has come to be seen as a human construct that is convened on the basis of a social contract that promises equal benefit to all who join. Among other things, this understanding of the church's nature has redefined the pastor's job description along the lines of therapist, teacher, and CEO.

Individualism and consumerism have also influenced our perception of the church's *purpose*, especially with respect to worship, discipleship, and witness. The modern "worship service" is driven by the ideal, "promise to meet their needs and they will come; meet their needs and they will stay." Likewise discipleship has become highly individualized. One can be a disciple of Christ and a member of the universal church without ever darkening the door of a local faith community. One's self-identify as a follower of Christ is informed more by the modern than the biblical narrative. Both liberal and conservative forms of Christian witness have come to see salvation as the eradication of sin – each espousing their own "gospel of sin management."

In the end, Christianity's withdrawal from mystery in the modern period is but a single chapter of the church's existence in the world. We may be tempted to criticize these developments as ill conceived and out of step with the Spirit's leading. But it is helpful to remember Jesus' promise: *the gates of Hades will never prevail against the church.* It is not ours to ask whether there might have been a better way for us to survive the modern age. We did what we did, Christ never left us, and we are still here. But the church, like Israel of old, does not stand still. The Big Bang of Pentecost impels us forward into the future, toward the end of the age. In the next chapter I offer a word of hope. Despite our faults and failures, Christ will never leave us or forsake us. We are after all his body.

12. Church's Dual Citizenship

Christ loved the church and gave himself up for her to make her holy, cleansing her by the washing with water through the word, and to present her to himself as a radiant church, without stain or wrinkle or any other blemish, but holy and blameless.

Ephesians 5:25–27

You've got to love this in a God – consistently assembling the motleyest to bring into this lonely and frightening world, a commitment to caring and community. It's a centuries-long reality-show – Moses the stutterer, Rahab the hooker, David the adulterer, Mary the homeless teenager. Not to mention the mealy-mouthed disciples. Not to mention a raging insecure narcissist like me.

Anne Lamott, *Plan B, Further Thoughts on Faith*

The Ugly and the Beautiful

The juxtaposition of these statements by the apostle Paul and Anne Lamott seems a fitting way to frame my assessment of the modern church in the last chapter. In many ways the church is a mosaic of contradicting images and ideals, a strenuous assemblage of the motleyest of people from all walks of life – of heroes and harlots, poseurs and poets, artisans and assassins, jingoists and geniuses, and everything in between.

At the end of the day, what are we to make of the church and its speckled track record? History tells the story. At times the church has zigged into suffocating institutionalism when it should have zagged into life-giving charisma. It opted to invoke violence and oppression instead of peacemaking and grace giving. Sometimes it swerved into syncretism rather than staying the course of faithfulness. At other times, it chose the way of irrelevance in preference to redemptive cultural engagement. In a word, the church has often stumbled over its own feet and become, if we dare say, an embarrassment to the spiritually sensible – a reality-show of the most ungainly type.

The church has taken a number of wrong turns along the way. Threatened by an increase in doctrinal and ethical diversity, the church in the second century sought to stabilize its existence by invoking institutional structures, which were governed by certified clergy who alone had the right to administer baptism and communion, and without whom there could be no legitimate instance of Christian community.

By the Middle Ages the disconnect between clergy and laity had become so pronounced that church officials considered laity to be little more than an appendage of the true church. Accordingly, the clerical church had little concern for the spiritual formation of laypersons. In fact, with the exception of certain mystics, hermits, monastic orders, and various groups of enthusiasts (dubbed "heretics" by the dominant church),[1] the clergy was often more preoccupied with servicing the institution than promoting life in the Spirit.

But there is another side to this reality-show that must be accounted for – a side that is perceived only by those whose eyes and ears have been opened by the risen Christ. This is the world of redeemed reality, in which the church's lurid failings are blanched into oblivion by the all-consuming radiance of Christ's glory. On this side of reality all shadows vanish. The church glows, without stain or wrinkle, free of blame and blemish. Despite how things appear to the naked eye – unaided by faith – the church exists simultaneously in both domains.

Several years ago I had an experience at a Sunday morning worship service that forever changed the way I relate to the church. It brought home in the most unforgettable of ways the truth of the church's dual citizenship in these seemingly incompatible spheres. The stage is set in a school gymnasium where the church has gathered for its Sunday morning worship service. The elements of communion are being distributed, and I am at one of the darkest moments of my spiritual journey.

"The Body of Christ" – A Personal Story

I sat quietly as the time for communion came. Gentle music softened the atmosphere but did little to fill the emptiness in my soul. My chronic disappointment with God had left me resigned to what seemed an undeniable fact: *the church was simply a failure*. After enduring countless hurts and hard knocks over sixteen years of pastoral ministry, I was finally ready to have a candid but calm-headed conversation with God about his Great Mistake – the church. But the story starts earlier.

I entered the ministry in 1982 with high hopes of changing the world. The thought of spending all my time doing kingdom work energized me no end. My job with the *Los Angeles Times* had afforded a lot of flexibility in my daytime schedule, and I spent as much time as I could reading Scripture and serving the church. I could not wait to finish training and start my first ministry assignment. But something very strange happened when I made the move from volunteer church member to paid ministry leader.

It took almost ten years for me to realize why I struggled with such ambivalence toward my role as a pastor. Then, in a moment of clarity, I realized that something profound and unexpected had occurred. Before I went into full-time ministry I served the church out of love for Christ and his people. The church was an oasis of the soul, a refuge from the world and its ubiquitous pressures to perform and succeed. It never occurred to me that by entering the ministry I would be trading a safe place for a workplace, complete with a job description and high expectations of success – imposed by others and myself.

I became deeply depressed. I was haunted by feelings of inadequacy and guilt. The church was no longer an oasis. I recalled a warning that one of my professors issued repeatedly.

He said it was a bad idea to be friends with the people at church. "Familiarity breeds contempt," he said. "You'll lose your prophetic edge if you get too close to the members of the church."

But life in ministry was lonely and I found such advice confusing. I wondered, "If I can only be friends with people outside the church, what happens when they embrace Christ and start coming to church? Do I have to stop being their friend or tell them to go to another church?"

Nor was I prepared to cope with life on the holy pedestal. Perhaps in my younger days as a Roman Catholic I too had thought that priests were cut from different metaphysical cloth. But I had forgotten (or repressed) those ideas. I discovered afresh that many Christians and non-Christians think that pastors and ministry staff workers are *different*. People say things like, "I guess pastors are human too" – as if they were holding out an olive branch to make me feel better about myself. What am I to say? "Thanks for the extra grace. You are so kind. The truth is . . . most of the time *I am human*." Or perhaps I should respond, "Thank you for recognizing that I am human. That's so enlightened of you. You know most people assume I'm something else. Maybe it's because I leave no footprints when I walk in the sand." I came to realize that if a person felt compelled to say such a thing, it usually meant that they thought I was in some way ontologically distinct from the rest of the human race. Heaven forbid that I should get angry, say a curse word, or emit some unseemly bodily noise in public.

As the years in ministry went by, I experienced far more blessing than grief, but there was an abiding distaste for the church that would not go away. Then in 1997 there occurred a series of events that dispelled the ambivalence and left me with razor-sharp ire toward the church.

A successful business venture had brought an unexpected financial windfall to my family and me, which in turn spawned a spirit of jealousy and ill will among a few vocal parishioners. It had always been difficult for me to receive criticism, as it usually awakened my own insecurities and feelings of inadequacy. But at this point in my journey it simply made me angry.

I tendered my resignation with the offer of serving the church indefinitely without pay. Although the members of the board were disappointed with the decision, they agreed that I should continue my preaching ministry to give them time to figure out what to do next. One board member, who was apparently envious of our good fortune, strongly objected to the prospect of my remaining in a position of pastoral leadership without remuneration. He reasoned, "If we can't pay him, we can't control him. And if we can't control him, who knows what he might do?" He asked me flat out, "Just what *are* your intentions anyway?" "Bill," I said (not his real name), "you've known me for six years. Have I ever given you reason to think that I would have some sinister plan?" He was convinced that the swift change in our financial standing had caused me to become a different person. I was heartsick. The other board members appeared unable (or unwilling) to convince him otherwise. Then came the worst church business meeting of my life.

A year earlier I had hired a worship leader to assist a very conflicted "praise team." Throughout the six years I had served that church, the worship ministry had been more troublesome than all the other ministries combined. At the heart of the turmoil were two headstrong women who had systematically alienated everyone whose musical talents, charisma, or leadership skills surpassed their own. The new worship leader had a lot of experience with such groups and knew exactly how to handle the situation. Within six months, the two problem individuals had left to serve other ministries and the group enjoyed a season of much-needed peace.

However, because the hiring of a worship leader posed a significant financial challenge, we agreed to raise funds to cover his salary for one year and then decide toward the end of that time whether to keep him on and absorb his salary into the budget. The majority of the members were pleased to see this man become a permanent fixture of the pastoral staff. And, as is often the case, those who were most happy demonstrated their support by not attending the business meeting – and that provided an opportunity for the unhappy minority to exert a disproportionate degree of influence.

Unbeknownst to the elders and pastoral staff, one of the women who had been displaced from the worship team conducted a telephone campaign before the meeting. Every person who had a beef with the worship leader or who was less than satisfied with his choice of music was encouraged to attend the meeting and vote against the proposal to keep him on. As soon as the meeting started it became apparent that trouble was afoot. But the elder chairing the proceedings did little to quell the controversy. I was neutralized at the outset of the meeting when he acknowledged my presence as "the lame-duck pastor."

Open dialog quickly became openly hostile. The worship leader was put on the defensive. Several unpleasant exchanges occurred between this man and some irritated members. Then the elder chairing the meeting asked the worship leader to leave the building, which gave naysayers all the more incentive to vent their feelings without being challenged. It was obvious that some were willing to sacrifice anything and anybody to have church *their way*.

The votes were cast. Despite the controversy, the majority voted to make the worship leader a permanent member of the pastoral staff. One of the dissenters immediately brandished a copy of the church bylaws. He cited the paragraph that stipulated the need for a supermajority when voting on paid positions in the church. The vote had passed by a slim margin – 53%. Then, in the most unbelievable turn of events, the elder in charge of the meeting said, "Well I guess that settles it. The vote to have the worship leader continue to serve this church has been defeated. He is hereby terminated."

The members who did not attend the meeting were appalled when they found out what had happened. They called for another meeting to rescind the decision and take another vote. But in the meantime the worship leader's wife had accepted an invitation to become the principal of a school outside the area. She had received the offer a week before, and the two had been prayerfully waiting on the outcome of the meeting to decide what to do. They had already put their house up for rent and started to pack their belongings. There was no undoing what had been done.

When the church gathered for worship the next Sunday, a brave volunteer clumsily played his guitar and led the singing. The hole left by the worship leader was like a vortex that sucked everything into its center. The service was languid and dirge-like. Grief and anger intermingled with triumphal smugness, frothing a noxious brew of animosity. Two sorts of faces met mine that day when I stood to preach – some conveyed the scornful message, "I got my way and there's nothing you can do about it." The majority of faces, however, were drawn and forlorn, communicating plaintively, "What do we do now?"

I was faced with a choice. The majority would have jumped at the chance to leave the curmudgeons to their own devices and start a new church. But I had preached for years that when conflict arises, we must not run from it. Christ calls us into redemptive community that is tested and strengthened by differences and discord. What holds the body of Christ together, I would say, is the fact that the One who unifies the church is far greater than anything or anyone that might try to divide it. But then in the crucible of anger and pain, I realized that it is far easier to preach that message than it is to live it.

In the moments before I spoke, I thought of how good it would feel to say something like, "A great injustice has been perpetrated upon this congregation by a few self-centered, stiff-necked ne'er-do-wells that are neither concerned for the welfare of Christ's church or interested in reaching out to the world. They have sinned – and unless they repent and apologize for their actions, we should decide here and now to put them out of our midst or to leave this place and start a new church." But I knew that something far more important – though less scintillating than my imagined comments – was called for that day.

I drew a deep breath, held it for a moment, then spoke: "As a church family, we are confronted with an opportunity that hasn't come along at any other time since I have been your pastor. We stand at a crossroads. We can either seize the opportunity to prove that we are the body of Christ, and show the world that Jesus Christ is Lord, or we can prove that there's no difference between us and any other social-service agency."

I then had the congregation read John 13:33–35, in which Jesus says:

> My children, I will be with you only a little longer. You will look for me, and just as I told the Jews, so I tell you now: Where I am going, you cannot come. A new command I give you: Love one another. As I have loved you, so you must love one another. By this everyone will know that you are my disciples, if you love one another.

I emphasized verse 35, which underscores the fact that the most powerful proof of an authentic relationship with Jesus Christ is our love for each other. Then I said, "The one thing that proves the mettle of true, Christlike love and distinguishes it from its unregenerate look-alike is conflict. Love is only tested and authenticated when we're not getting along with each other. It's only when our feelings are hurt and we're riven by disagreement and anger that the unifying power of true love takes over and holds us together."

Then I directed the congregation to John 17:20–23, in which Jesus prays for all believers:

> My prayer is not for them alone. I pray also for those who will believe in me through their message, that all of them may be one, Father, just as you are in me and I am in you. May they also be in us so that the world may believe that you have sent me. I have given them the glory that you gave me, that they may be one as we are one: I in them and you in me. May they be brought to complete unity to let the world know that you sent me and have loved them even as you have loved me.

I pointed out that Jesus was speaking of a unity that is visible to the world, not the abstract unity of the "church universal," construed in all of its variegated forms. Moreover, it is *abnormal unity* that points unmistakably to its supernatural source – proof positive that the Father sent Jesus to be the Savior of the world. I said that the most compelling evidence we can offer the world regarding the truthfulness of the gospel is a church filled with people who have no earthly reason to love each other the way they do – but still do; who have no basis to hang together other than the unifying reality of the risen Christ.

I continued, "Some in this congregation have acted in ways that were very hurtful. But the question we must now answer is not who is right or who is wrong. The question is whether we can forgive those who've wronged us and seek forgiveness from those we've wronged. The question is whether we can see this time for what it truly is – a time to be conduits through which God's grace flows to each other; a time to love one another and stick together when it makes no earthly sense to do so; a time to *be the body of Christ.*"

Both sorts of faces softened as I spoke, communicating a willingness to embrace the opportunity to be the church in that time and place. We turned a corner that day. What could have shattered the church ended up making it stronger. Our problems did not disappear by any means, but for a season at least, everyone together caught a glimpse of the One who loves unceasingly and thereupon incorporates us into the perfection of Trinitarian unity. To a person, we went away from that service with the realization that being the body of Christ is about much more than receiving grace – it is about living out our redemption through giving grace to each other precisely when we do not deserve it.

Now, many years later, that congregation is thriving. Its membership is strong and a few years back it completed construction on a new and much larger facility located on one of the town's main thoroughfares.

At the time, however, celebration was nowhere on the horizon. The pain and anger I was feeling at that time blinded me to the victory won against the forces of darkness. It took several years for me to realize that the church's staying together through that storm marked a high point of my ministry. Three months later the elders thanked me for my service and the congregation gave my family and me a going-away party and a nice plaque. We started attending another church in the area where a good friend was the pastor – and I entered what would prove to be a four-year dark night of the soul that left me spiritually disenfranchised from the church. At the outset of this dark night I said to Dianne, "I will continue to attend church for your sake and for the sake of our children, but so far as I am concerned, I am dead to the church and the church is dead to me."

During the next four years I was able to hide this dark night from most people. But Dianne knew. And she grieved over the fact that the joy and camaraderie we shared in ministry had faded into distant memory. One year into the dark night I moved to George Fox Evangelical Seminary to serve as a professor and administrator. In my work with colleagues and students, I rediscovered a long-lost oasis of the soul. But during the first three years there – though few were aware of it – I was afflicted with deep-seated antipathy toward the church, which, without warning would burst through the thin veneer of my pious façade like a volcanic eruption. I wondered if I would ever again be alive to the church.

The Body of Christ

This brings us full circle – to the communion service. My family and I had just begun a courtship with a church whose youth group had attracted our teenaged children. Just before the worship service started I attempted to say good morning to a couple of people standing at the back of the gymnasium. Although they both clearly heard my greeting, neither was willing to make eye contact or even acknowledge the gesture. The thin veneer started to buckle. I sat down and thought to myself, "What's wrong with the church? People are so self-absorbed that they can't even say hello to a visitor . . . *who is trying to say hello to them!*" The service got underway and soon it was time for communion.

I was bemused at the way this group chose to practice Eucharist. After a brief prayer trays containing the symbols of

Christ's body and blood were passed unceremoniously to the congregation – one right after the other. Canned background music emanated from ill-tuned speakers while each congregant was left to self-commune, deciding for oneself at what point along the way to consume the bread and juice . . . in time enough to beat the prayer for the offering I waited for the trays to reach my row. With one eye half opened I quietly prayed, "O God, what were you thinking when you created the church? Its track record speaks for itself."

I began to reflect on the conflicts and failures of the church over the centuries – of its struggles with divergent teachings and the emergence of church government that matched the hierarchical structure of the Roman government; of Caesaropapism (the combining of secular and spiritual authority) and its devastating consequences, which infected the church from Constantine on; of the Great Schism between the church of the East and West; of the medieval, Spanish, and Roman inquisitions; of the Crusades and their cruel effects on Europe, the Islamic world, and the Jewish community; of the conquistadors who savagely killed, enslaved, and raped in the name of Christ; of the bloody and barbaric persecution of Anabaptists by both Catholics and Protestants; of the Salem witch burnings in the North and the owning of slaves in the South. I thought of the church's prevailing narcissism; of its cultural irrelevance and spiritual anemia. By now the elements of the Eucharist were coming my way.

I grasped a morsel of bread and plastic cup from the passing trays. The bread fragment was shaped like a Tylenol caplet, white and hard, like a pellet. With little forethought I placed the pill between my lips and pulverized it with my front teeth – *chomp, chomp, chomp* – like a rabbit. It was dry, tasteless, and gritty. As I ground the bread capsule with my teeth, it formed an unsavory paste in my mouth. I rolled my eyes and whispered to myself, *"The body of Christ! A perfect metaphor."* Words scarcely convey what happened next.

A voice softly spoke inside my mind. At first I thought it was a product of my own imagination, but the more I listened, the more I realized I had no control over what it said.

"This is my body. Sometimes my body is dry and lifeless – completely self-absorbed and spiritually dead.

"This is my body. Sometimes my body is tasteless and anything but what it should be to the world.

"This is my body. Sometimes my body is gritty, profoundly hurting its own."

At that point I was simply listening. The words were strangely at home in my mind and yet seemed to be coming from somewhere else. I was more intrigued than frightened. The voice was gentle and peace inducing.

Then came the unexpected:

"And when you love my body, you love me the way I love you."

Scales fell from my eyes and for the first time I was able to see things as they had always been – the church simultaneously occupying both realities . . . with me as one of the motleyest of its members. A soul-renewing truth became crystal clear: *Jesus Christ sacramentally presents himself to us in the imperfections of his body so that we might love him as he loves us.*

Conclusion

Since that time I have celebrated the mystery that an imperfect church is none other than Christ the Lord, presenting himself to us in human infirmity, which he atoned for on the cross, intercedes for in glory, and will transform at the consummation of the age. We are not to resent the church for its foibles, for the church's present state grants us the priceless opportunity to love Christ in his disfigurement as he loves us in ours. When we love the church in its imperfections, we experience a level of reciprocity and intimacy with Christ that can be had in no other way. In this juxtaposition of seemingly opposite realities, we are awakened to a truth of Copernican implications – irrespective of its failings past, present, or future, the church is the body of Christ – *broken for us.*

13. What Now?

LORD, *I know that people's lives are not their own; it is not for them to direct their steps. Discipline me, LORD, but only in due measure – not in your anger, or you will reduce me to nothing.*

Jeremiah 10:23, 24, TNIV

God will send out his Spirit and the waters will flow once more. What before was stone is turned into pools of water; the hardest granite is now a splashing fountain.

Gregory of Nyssa, *On the Song of Songs*

Accepting our Imperfect Status

Deficiencies of the soul are certainly nothing to revel in, but neither are they something to run from. Some day the church will be perfect, but not today. At some point we will be completely formed in Christ, but not right now. It is a matter of faith to accept the fact that the only place to meet Christ and celebrate our joint fellowship in the atonement is now, in the present. We cannot transport ourselves to some idyllic place past or future. We are most fully the church, most completely formed in Christ when we are wholly present to his presence in the here and now.

I mentioned earlier that I am uneasy with the proposal that conceives the way of Christ as the recovery of some long-lost pristine age, where the church had it right and Christian life and doctrine were pure. I am equally troubled by those who are so focused on future events that they spend an inordinate amount of time reading the book of Revelation in one hand and the newspaper in the other, hoping to add yet another piece to their apocalyptic puzzle. Both approaches run the risk of fruitless preoccupation and seem to arise out of a common, modern restlessness with the present. Even the so-called emergent church is fixated on "ancient–future" forms of worship. But we must ask, "Where is Christ if not in the present?"

Theologian Ray Anderson used to trick his doctoral students from time to time by asking a question whose answer seemed obvious enough. "Which century," he would ask, "is determinative as a context for our understanding of biblical truth?" Most of his students were seminary graduates and practicing pastors, so they felt qualified to answer the question with little forethought. "Why, the first century, of course," they would say. They bolstered their claim by reminding Dr. Anderson that biblical scholars have gone to great lengths to ascertain the contextual factors of the biblical world in order to aid in our understanding of the text.

Anderson would then ask a follow-up question. "Does this mean that the context of first-century Christianity is normative for our understanding of what it means to live and minister according to biblical truth?" Without fail his students would respond in the affirmative. Then he would set the hook: "*I do not agree!*" He would go on to explain that when we embrace Christ in faith, we receive the indwelling gift of the Holy Spirit in anticipation of Christ's return. The Spirit is a "pledge" or "down payment" of our ultimate inheritance in Christ. "When Christ returns to bring to consummation this pledge made by the gift of the Holy Spirit," says Anderson, "it will be the 'last century.' The Spirit is thus preparing the people of God for this 'last century.'" Accordingly, "we should expect that the Spirit will more and more prepare the church to be the church that Christ desires to see when he returns, not the one that he left in the first century."[1]

Anderson's point sounds just the right note for those of us who want to be faithful to the way of Christ in the world. The Spirit of Christ meets us where we're at and impels us toward the glorious future that he has prepared for us. The church has had its failings. No sensible Christian will deny that fact. Nor should we assume that this will stop being the case until Christ returns. But failings notwithstanding, the One who *was* and *is to come* is also the One who *is*. He is *Immanuel* – "God with us," our ever-present help who joins us in the journey right now and enables us to locate ourselves in his grand salvation story. There is a direct correlation between our spiritual health and the degree to which we effectively attend, perceive, and respond to our present Lord. Faithfulness isn't perfection. We will probably get some things wrong in the process of trying to sort out how best to be the people of God in our generation. But like our faithful sisters and brothers of past generations, we must give it our best shot and trust that God's love will cover the multitude of mistakes we make along the way. It rests with the historians of future generations to judge how well we did in this endeavor.

We've had to contend with two very powerful forces in the practice of Christian community – individualism and its evil twin, consumerism. At this point, we have gained just enough ground to see a few specific ways in which our practices as the church have conformed to the pattern of the world, instances in which there was a bit too much accommodation to culture. By far the majority of Christians in the West have not gone so far in their accommodation to culture to lose their way completely. Still, our spiritual vitality, intimacy with Christ, and witness in the world have suffered measurably. But there is a difference between being unduly influenced by culture and being unfaithful to Jesus Christ.

Faithful Development

Contrary to the claims of some contemporary thinkers, I maintain that the church in the modern West never ceased being the church in its adaptation to cultural categories. Our history proves that adapting to culture is in fact the only viable option. Gerald R. McDermott accurately observes that both Israel and the church drew widely from their contemporary surroundings as they described their experiences and formulated doctrine.[2] He points out several instances in both Hebrew and New Testament Scripture in which the biblical writers made careful but liberal use of their cultural categories. Quoting Andrew Walls, McDermott says that Christianity is in principle "the most syncretistic religion in the world." For God chose "to reveal his truth gradually through time rather than in one blinding and all-encompassing flash of revelation . . ." He argues that God has always used religious and philosophical systems outside his covenant people "to help unfold and interpret his reality."[3] To deny this divine pattern, says McDermott, is to run the risk of substituting ideology for theology.[4]

What changes in every instance of healthy development is not the essence of Christianity itself, for such a thing never exists apart from its embodiedness in human life. Theologian Thomas Oden points out that the way we understand and express Christian "doctrine" does not mean that we alter the substance of doctrine in each new age. What it means, he says, is "addressing the changing vitalities of each new historical situation with the original apostolic tradition." Doing this both imaginatively and faithfully is the ongoing challenge of ministry. It is a challenge that Irenaeus, Augustine, Nicholas of Cusa, Calvin, and Teresa of Avila have all shared in immensely different historical settings.[5] This is what Christianity did in its modern setting. The creative appropriation of Western categories reflects the same developmental practice that the church has always used.

Our engagement with culture tends to occur in fits and starts. Sometimes we embrace culture a bit too much; at other times we retreat from it more than we should. Jim McClendon comments on this phenomenon. He says that the church's fluctuation between engaging with culture and withdrawing from culture is like the diastolic–systolic rhythm of a healthy beating heart. He made this observation as he concluded his life's work as a theologian. Suffering from congestive heart failure with only a few months to live, McClendon felt a deep sense of solidarity with the church he spent his life serving. In search of "a single lively metaphor" to capture well his life's work, he found what he was looking for in the writings of Edwin Ewart Aubrey and Julian Hartt.

Both writers used the metaphor of a beating heart, but they did so differently. Aubrey drew upon this image to describe the alternation between periods in which the church reaches out to absorb elements of culture, which it uses to enrich its life and thought, and periods in which it "draws into itself in a contractive movement, which tries to exclude cultural forces so as to recover its own uniqueness."[6] Hartt used the same image to describe the church's rhythm of going out into the world to serve and returning again to worship and reflect.[7]

McClendon wondered how these two seemingly conflicting uses of the same metaphor might both be true of the church. Then it occurred to him that he had overlooked a basic fact of human (and animal) circulation – both of these phenomena occur at the same time in every heartbeat:

> The same systolic contraction of the heart that drives blood out to the body's members simultaneously pumps blood through another artery into the lungs, where its impurities are removed and fresh oxygen is acquired. The same diastolic relaxation and enlargement of the heart, thanks to its cleverly divided chambers, at once permits matter drawn through veins from all parts of the body to the heart *and* through another great vessel permits fresh, lung-purified blood to enter another of the heart's chambers.[8]

He goes on to say that if either of these processes fails, the heart fails and the body dies.

Taking our cue from McClendon, we could say that the church in its present state is "between heartbeats," at the seemingly tenuous midpoint between diastole and systole – at once ready to *take in* and *expel* contemporary culture; at once positioned to *serve* the world and *retreat* to the sanctuary (or study). This is evident in how we are greeting the many new changes in our cultural situation.

The Emergence of a New Era

Those of us in the West are entering a new chapter of our story, but we must resist the temptation to name what still defies a unified description. If there is one thing in particular that can be said about the present time, it is that *there is no one thing in particular that can be said about the present time.* Ours is a time of fluctuation and transition. It is ill advised to ascribe a single definition to our age, such as "postmodern," which implies that everything we call by that name is joined by some common denominator.[9] The further we go into the present age, the more apparent it becomes that the term "postmodern" has little if any descriptive value.[10] In fact to many in their twenties and thirties the term has become a sort of shibboleth – if we describe ourselves as "postmodern," it is most likely the case that we are *not*. Perhaps the most we can say about the present age is that it is in the process of *becoming* whatever it will be. Therefore the term *"emerging age"* is about the best we can do.[11] It falls to our great, great grandchildren to decide if any other appellation is warranted.

Radio, television, and the Internet have brought the global village into the living room of Western civilization, rousing us from our imperialistic slumber and forcing us to reckon with the fact that together we see the world in vastly different ways. Even though the world has been very diverse since the tower of Babel, the realization of this fact did not start to sink into our collective consciousness in the West until the latter part of the twentieth century. The net effect of this belated awareness, in its best form, has been increased tolerance for cultural and ethnic diversity and openness to alternative reality narratives beyond that of modern science.

A Divided House

The Western church has responded in two very different ways to its emerging context. Some are happy to be liberated from the burden of rational justification and anxious to engage in new forms of cultural expression in worship, discipleship, and witness. Others are deeply troubled. They recoil at the idea that human knowledge is socially conditioned and fear that to accept such a proposal is to take the first step onto the slippery slope of relativism.[12] If our so-called knowledge of spiritual truth is nothing more than the product of the group's "shared perspective," they ask, what hope in there of knowing truth at all?

The church in the twenty-first century is at a crossroads, with some wanting to dive headlong into the emerging age and others unwilling to surrender their stake in modernity's firm foundation. Those of the former persuasion accuse the latter of being narrow-minded modernists who simply don't get it. Those of the latter category accuse the former of selling their birthright of Christian truth for a bowl of postmodern stew. Both sides often talk past each other – neither hearing nor being understood (or valued) by the other.[13]

Sadly, at a time when the wheat of the Western world has never been more ready for harvest, the church appears to be stuck in an ideological tug-of-war – and neither side appears to be able to offer a satisfactory alternative to a culture that is hungry for a taste of authentic Christian spirituality. On the one hand, the "emergent church" is strongly attracted to ancient–future forms of worship.[14] However, without sufficient discernment, such interests will be driven more by the consumerist appetite for novelty than by the desire to recapture the powerful practices of past generations that were buried under the sands of the modern age. "Anti-postmodern" Christians, on the other hand, are highly suspicious of emergent trends, preferring instead to protect the faith from the corrupting influences of an "age without reason." However, they have opted to do so by adhering to modes of social and doctrinal expression that are becoming less and less interesting to people in an emerging age.

It remains to be seen if we are, as some emerging-church representatives claim, witnessing another revolutionary phase of the church's existence – a new reformation – which, they say, comes around roughly every 500 years. That may be the case. Or, in an ironic déjà vu of the last century, we may be revisiting the well-worn paths that our liberal and fundamentalist brothers and sisters took at the beginning of the twentieth century. While so-called emergent Christians are anxious to pour the gospel into new cultural wineskins, anti-postmodern Christians are ready to hunker down and fight for Truth. This current state of affairs begs the question: *Where in the world is the church?*

Spiritual but not Religious

While Christians are at loggerheads over how best to engage culture, the atmosphere of the twenty-first-century Western world has become much more receptive to mystery. It is no longer necessary to convince people that there are many aspects of reality that are inaccessible to reason. The majority of people these days take that as a given, which is demonstrated by the growing openness to a wide variety of spiritual experiences. But this trend comes with a twist: to be "spiritual" is good, but to be "religious" is not. As many as half of all unchurched Americans identify themselves as "spiritual but not religious."[15] To those with an emerging twenty-first-century outlook, religion spells *institution* – and institution spells *oppression, greed*, and *manipulation*. "Organized religion" is taken to embody all that was wrong with the modern world. Ironically, however, the same people have warm feelings toward religious traditions whose roots go deep into antiquity. They are fascinated by longstanding religious traditions that have managed to weather the storms of the modern period, unsullied by the corrupting influences of modernity's political imperialism, corporate greed, and religious iconoclasm. The stigma associated with organized religion, at least in some circles, appears to be limited to modern forms of religious institution.

Robert C. Fuller cites an important study conducted by 346 social scientists representing a range of religious backgrounds. Their goal was to clarify what people mean when they say they're spiritual but not religious. The study revealed that most spiritual-but-not-religious people ascribe negative connotations to the term "religious," associating it with such things as church attendance, the clergy, and adherence to traditional beliefs. "Spiritual people," on the other hand, reject traditional forms of religion in favor of mysticism and nontraditional beliefs and practices. They are less likely, the study concludes,

> to engage in traditional forms of worship such as church attendance and prayer, less likely to engage in group experiences related to spiritual growth, more likely to be agnostic, more likely to characterize religiousness and spirituality as different and nonoverlapping concepts, more likely to hold nontraditional beliefs, *and more likely to have had mystical experiences.*[16]

Fuller goes on to note that many in this category claim that they've had off-putting experiences with churches and their leaders at some point – experiences ranging from unsavory encounters with hypocritical and self-serving attitudes to emotional and sexual abuse. Moreover, in comparison to their churchgoing counterparts, these spiritual seekers are more likely to be college-educated, white-collar, and politically liberal. They are less likely to have been raised by churchgoing parents and are generally less dependent on social relationships. Nevertheless, while quantitative data show how the spiritual but not religious differ from churchgoers socially and economically, it is difficult to understand, says Fuller, "how unchurched Americans assemble various bits and pieces of spiritual philosophy into a meaningful whole."[17]

Perhaps one reason why it is so difficult to identify how spiritual-but-not-religious people "assemble various bits and pieces" into "a meaningful whole" is because most of these people are not interested in meaningful wholes.[18] This concern, it appears to me, is more reflective of the researchers' interests than the actual behavior of those who claim to be spiritual but not religious. If there is any constant to be observed among these people, it is that their disaffection with institutional religion has left them far more receptive to mystery, which by its very nature resists reconciliation and synthesis.

Many of these seekers consider organized religion to have gone the way of the dodo and, in the absence of institutional religion and its dogmas, mystery is all that matters. The only question is where they will look for it – and the answer is, *anywhere they can find it*. A search of eBay's offerings reveals an insatiable hunger to possess and participate in mystery. The spiritual but not religious are looking for bits and pieces of mystery in a wide variety of forms, ranging from jewelry and clothing to religious artifacts like chalices, crucifixes, rosaries, offering plates, and works of art that are hundreds of years old in some cases – and herein lies an opportunity for the discerning church. The question, however, is whether the church will recognize these possibilities for what they really are and position itself to make good use of them.

Our spiritual-but-not-religious friends are presenting us with a Mars Hill opportunity. Like the Apostle Paul, we have the chance to give a name to their unknown god. But this opportunity also calls upon us to demonstrate the specific ways in which our experiences of mystery converge with theirs. A number of years ago I attended a workshop that was conducted by a well-known worship leader. At one point he made an unforgettable statement that has universal implications: "You cannot lead others where you are not going yourself." The only way to lead spiritual-but-not-religious people into "the glorious riches of this mystery, which is Christ in us, the hope of glory" (Colossians 1:27) is to participate in this glorious mystery ourselves.

14. The Way of Mystery

Don't become so well-adjusted to your culture that you fit into it without even thinking. Instead, fix your attention on God. You'll be changed from the inside out.

Romans 12:2a, *The Message*

Life is always more mysterious and less manageable than our theories about life – including our religious theories and systems of theology.

Douglas John Hall, *God and Human Suffering*

Zen and the Art of Motorcycle Riding

A few years back I arrived at work and found a large poster fixed to my office door. It pictured a man riding a Harley-Davidson down an open road. The caption read, "It's not the destination, it's the journey." Later that day I discovered that the phantom placard placer was none other than Chuck Church, the head librarian. I'm the only one at George Fox University's Portland Center Campus that rides a Harley. He figured I'd like the poster. I did. It stayed on my office door for two years.

I've been riding motorcycles for the better part of my life. Why I do not know. My parents had no interest in two-wheeled motorized vehicles. In fact when I was young they warned me about the perils of motorcycles. They recounted horror stories of people they knew who were maimed or killed while riding them. Still, on Christmas morning of my eleventh year they finally succumbed to my unending pleas and gave me a mini-bike – a Taco 22 with a three-horsepower Briggs and Stratton lawnmower engine. That was the beginning. Since then I've owned seven motorcycles. I currently ride a 1993 Ultra Classic Electra Glide – 90th Anniversary Edition.

There are basically two kinds of recreational motorcycle riders – crazies and cruisers. Crazies have a need for speed, and they like their bikes fast – with rocket-like acceleration and top speeds that make the police think their radar has locked onto a low-flying aircraft. Crazies are constantly pushing the limits of their machines, their skills, and their luck. Eventually no less than 50 percent of all such cyclists are killed or seriously injured while riding. For them the temptation to go fast is simply too much to resist. Cruisers, on the other hand, ride for reasons other than an adrenaline rush. Some do it for social reasons. Cruisers often ride with friends or in large groups. Others ride to enjoy the scenery. Cruisers love to travel on quiet roads and enjoy the beauty of uninhabited spaces. While crazies like their bikes light and fast, cruisers prefer machines that are heavy and stable. My bike weighs 800 pounds and its acceleration and top speed are dismally unimpressive to those of a more thrill-seeking nature. But that's not to say that cruisers don't risk their lives when they ride.

Two of my beloved friends, Dan and his father, Ray, began Saturday, October 29, 2005 like any other southern California weekend. The weather was perfect for a motorcycle ride, but Dan was having trouble with his Electra Glide Classic. It had been in and out of the shop, but the problem persisted. Dan asked his dad for some help and the two worked on the bike through the better part of the morning. Ray was a seasoned mechanic in his early seventies. The repair went smoothly and successfully. The two men decided to go for a short ride – Dan on his Harley and Ray on his.

Ray cannot tell us why he went wide on his last turn. It appears to have been momentary inattention. The two had just set out for Julian, a quaint town in the Cuyamaca mountain range known for its apples. It was to have been a short ride. They were just a few miles from home. All Dan remembers is the sound – he can't get it out of his mind. Nor can he erase the image of his dad's body flying through the air. Ray was catapulted from his motorcycle after colliding head on with a car traveling in the other direction. He landed more than sixty feet from the point of impact. He was life-flighted to the hospital. The doctors and medical personnel did their best to save him, but he suffered massive internal injuries. A few hours later Ray met his Savior.

I cannot speak for Ray, but I can say that nearly every close call I've had riding a motorcycle was the result of being distracted. Motorcycle riding, to be safe, has to be Zen. I'm not the first to see the connection between Zen and motorcycles. Robert M. Pirsig articulated this connection in his 1974 book, *Zen and the Art of Motorcycle Maintenance.* What's distinctive about Zen Buddhism is the way it uniquely focuses one's attention on the now. Tucker N. Callaway was a Christian missionary to Japan. In his excellent book, *Zen Way, Jesus Way,* Callaway adeptly uncovers the mysteries of Zen in a way that is surprisingly accessible to Westerners.[1] He says that Zen Buddhists conceive of reality in a way that is virtually unfathomable to those of us in the West.

The best way to understand the Zen mind, says Callaway, is by means of an analogy. According to Zen Buddhism, reality as we know it does not exist. It is the figment of our collective imaginations. Picture a film projector, with upper and lower reels. What we experience in the now is the image of the single frame that's projected through the lens as it passes from the upper reel of "stored-up consciousness" to the lower reel of "stored-up memory." The unenlightened spend their time either reminiscing about what has already passed into stored-up memory or speculating on what might be ahead in stored-up consciousness. Neither the past nor future is real, however. It's an illusion of the unenlightened mind.

Enlightenment occurs by means of becoming so fixated on the single frame of film in front of the lens – so focused on *the now* – that all illusions vanish. Locked in the suspended animation of that single frame, frozen between stored-up consciousness and stored-up memory, the Zen Buddhist existentially encounters the unmediated secret of all that falsely claims to be real. For Zen Buddhists, what's "really real" is *Mu*, which means "nothing." The "Buddha mind," or enlightenment, occurs when the Zen Buddhist by means of meditation enters upon ultimate nothingness, *Mu*, the pure non-reality behind all that masks itself as real.

Callaway acknowledges that the Zen way of construing reality is a far cry from the biblical witness. But he says that if our perspective as followers of Christ can benefit at all from Zen Buddhism, it is precisely in this practice of engaging the present rather than being so focused on the past or future that we are inattentive to God's presence in the here and now. Harley-Davidson's watchword is apropos: "It's not the destination, it's the journey." Being present to the present moment of our journey is what Zen and the art of motorcycle riding have in common. You need complete focus on the immediacy of the moment to be an enlightened Zen and a safe and happy motorcycle rider, whether you're a crazy or a cruiser. And, as we will see shortly, it is the only way to engage mystery in the Christian life.

The Distraction of Clarity

In his book, *Ruthless Trust*, acclaimed author and speaker Brennan Manning describes an exchange between Mother Teresa and John Kavanaugh. Vexed about what to do with his life, Kavanaugh had volunteered to spend three months with the mystic, ministering to Calcutta's sick and dying. On the first day he met with Mother Teresa and implored her to pray that he might have clarity about the future. To his dismay she refused, saying it was the last thing he needed. He countered by saying that all he wanted was the same sort of clarity he witnessed in her. Mother Teresa laughed out loud and said, "I have never had clarity; what I have always had is trust." She told Kavanaugh that she would pray for him to trust God rather than have clarity.[2]

The pursuit of clarity leads to spiritual myopia. We followers of Christ are very good at spiritualizing what is so patently earthly – the attempt to live by our own wits and

satisfy our own pleasures. The lust for clarity is a disease
of the soul whose symptoms, ironically, include much talk
about knowing and doing the will of God. "But wait a
minute!" someone will object. "Aren't we supposed to know
and obey God's will?" The answer of course is yes. But the
problem is a matter of focus – hence the myopia. Instead
of concentrating our discernment focus on Christ, we are
focused on ourselves and a given set of desired outcomes.

Clarity leaves no place for faith. Scripture actually
contrasts faith and clarity – "we live by faith, not by sight"
(2 Corinthians 5:7). This is where we see the true colors of
the quest for clarity. To have clarity is to be certain; it is to
have confidence that we are on the right course; it is to see
the goal. Like the unenlightened Buddhist who's mesmerized
by the reels instead of the single frame; like the motorcyclist
who takes his eyes off the road for a fleeting-but-deadly
second, the pursuit of certainty is a distraction that directs
our focus away from the immediacy of Jesus' presence in our
lives.

The distraction of clarity is even evident in many late-
twentieth-century books on spiritual discernment. Rather than
inviting us to experience the immediacy of Jesus' presence,
many authors equate discernment with decision-making.[3]
This has been the case even among the Friends, for whom
discernment has been central to their gathered experience.[4]
The focus of discernment-as-decision-making is on *making
the right choice* and *realizing the desired outcome*. Those who
are fixated on clarity, in other words, are focused on the
destination rather than the journey.

Living Sacrifices

Scripture calls us to engage in a very different sort of practice
– a discipline that empowered the lives of mystics like Mother
Teresa and Brother Lawrence. It is the way of *clearness in the
moment* rather than clarity about the future. The Apostle Paul
describes this practice in Romans 12. Mind you, this comes
right after his doxological aha! moment that appears at the

close of chapter 11. In the immediate context, the apostle has just finished a reflection on God's sovereign disposition of mercy toward Jews and non-Jews. More broadly, chapter 11 marks the close of an extended reflection on the outworking of God's grace through the "good news" of Christ, which is "the power of God that brings salvation to everyone who believes: first to the Jew, then to the Gentile" (Romans 1:16).

There are different theories about biblical inspiration. The verbal dictation theory envisions the Holy Spirit sitting on the writer's shoulder, giving the scribe the exact words to be recorded. The so-called "mantic theory" sees the writer temporarily "possessed" by the Holy Spirit, rendering the scribe completely unconscious to his or her own thoughts and impulses. Neither view is very popular today. More reasoned theories try to account for the distinctively human characteristics that are preserved in Scripture. The personalities, emotions, and vocabularies of the writers are evident throughout the Bible, including the book of Romans.

Novelist Edgar Lawrence Doctorow once described writing as exploration. "You start from nothing," he said, "and learn as you go." I imagine that biblical writers, guided as they were by the Holy Spirit, often discovered new things as they wrote. It certainly seems that Paul was surprised and delighted by what he had just written. It evoked wondrous praise:

> Oh, the depth of the riches of the wisdom and knowledge of God!
>> How unsearchable his judgments,
>> and his paths beyond tracing out!
> "Who has known the mind of the Lord?
>> Or who has been his counselor?"
> "Who has ever given to God,
>> that God should repay them?"
> For from him and through him and to him are all things.
>> To him be the glory forever! Amen.
>
> (Romans 11:33–36, TNIV)

What struck Paul in that moment was the realization that God's ways are not our ways. God in his mercy is tenderly and powerfully orchestrating his world in ways that surpass human wisdom or comprehension. What we are to do in response to this realization is the subject of the rest of the epistle, beginning with the discernment practice described in Romans 12.

Paul employs priestly imagery to describe a life-transforming spiritual discipline by which we engage mystery in the Christian life. With our focus on God's tender mercies manifested in Christ, we are to offer our bodies as living sacrifices. The irony is obvious. Sacrifices in Hebrew Scripture were of necessity slaughtered before they were offered on the altar. We are not left to wonder what the apostle means here. He explains. Offering our bodies as living sacrifices is our "spiritual act of worship" (v. 2, NIV). Translators struggle with this phrase. Paul combines two concepts – the word from which we get "logic" or "reason" (*logikos*) and the term he uses in 9:4 to describe the daily activities of Jewish priests (*latreia*).[5]

From the days of Moses through King David, the priests tended to the daily duties of the *tabernacle*, a movable structure that was built according to the specifications that God disclosed to Moses on Mt. Sinai (see Exodus 25:9). These duties continued in the Jerusalem temple, which was first completed in 960 BC during the reign of King Solomon (see 1 Kings 6 – 8). The temple was destroyed by the Babylonians in 486 BC and rebuilt at least twice before it was finally destroyed by Rome in AD 70, ending the Jewish priesthood.

The daily activities of priests were anything but glamorous. Aside from the extra responsibilities associated with major Jewish feast days, priests had to watch over the fire on the altar to make sure it kept burning day and night. They had to keep the golden lampstand outside the veil alive with oil. They had to sacrifice two one-year-old lambs per day, one in the morning and the other in the evening. On top of these daily offerings were the many sacrifices that the people brought to the priests – burnt offerings, grain offerings, fellowship offerings, sin offerings, and guilt offerings. Priests had to teach Israelite children the statutes of the Lord. They had to play the role of judge and arbiter in civil proceedings, diagnose infectious skin diseases, and inspect people's homes for deadly mildew. And during the days of the wilderness wandering, it was the priests' responsibility to cover the Ark of the Covenant and all the vessels of the sanctuary with purple or scarlet cloth before they could be transported by their Levitical relatives. Priests toiled daily under the heat of the Middle Eastern sun, enduring the stench of curdled blood and fighting off the flies and vermin drawn to the animal carcasses. Their work was a day-in-day-out affair that was both difficult and monotonous.

The Apostle Paul ingeniously fuses two key concepts from the pagan and Jewish worlds – *logikos*, a favorite expression of Greek philosophers, and *latreia*, a word denoting in this context daily priestly service. Together these terms form one new meaning. We are envisioned as *both* the offerers and the offerings. *Logikos* describes how we offer ourselves and *latreia* identifies what of ourselves we offer – for we are in fact to be "living sacrifices." We offer ourselves *intentionally* and *consciously* (*logikos*). What we offer to God is *everything that makes up our daily lives* (*latreia*). In other words, we offer our bodies as living sacrifices by *consciously appropriating everything we are and do – in the here-and-now moment of daily living – to the glory of God*. Eugene Peterson captures well the meaning of this passage in his paraphrase, *The Message*: "Take your everyday, ordinary life – your sleeping, eating, going-to-work, and walking-around life – and place it before God as an offering."

This discipline requires us to be present to the moment, like good Zen monks and artful motorcycle riders. It beckons us away from the Sirens' call of clarity about the future and toward the discovery of mystery in the clearness of the moment. Offering ourselves to God in this way sharpens our spiritual intuition so that in every moment we happen to occupy we are "able to test and approve what God's will is – his good, pleasing and perfect will" (Romans 12:2).

The Revelation of Mystery

God doesn't keep secrets. While it is true, as Deuteronomy 29:29 attests, that the "secret things belong to the Lord" – in other words, there are some things that we will never be able to fathom this side of eternity – "the revealed things," as the passage goes on to say, "belong to us and to our children forever." The word "mystery" in Scripture does not describe some forbidden secret that is available only to the initiated, or to those who join a PhD program and sit with a group of misfits musing all day long about theology. "Mystery," to be sure, speaks of what is *hidden* or *secret*. But that is only half the equation. God is said to be "the revealer of mysteries" (Daniel 2:29).

In almost every instance of its use in Scripture, the term mystery also includes the fact of revelation. According to God's good pleasure, he made known to us the mystery, which he purposed in Christ (Ephesians 1:9). As St. Paul wrote of this mystery, he wanted to make sure that it was crystal clear to his readers (Ephesians 3:2–11). And he wanted us to pray for him so that he would "fearlessly make known the mystery of the gospel" whenever he opened his mouth (Ephesians 6:19). Although the mystery of the gospel was "hidden for ages and generations," it is now disclosed to the followers of Christ (Colossians 1:26). It is nothing less than "Christ in us, the hope of glory" (v. 27). In light of its use in Scripture, the following practical definition of the term seems fitting: *Mystery is something that was once concealed but is now revealed.*

Conclusion

The primary place of mystery is the *now* of daily life. Jesus is forever present to us, wrapped in the ongoing moment of daily existence. He longs for us to find him there and delights in us every time we do. He wants us to consecrate every waking moment to the awareness of his company. In fact, Jesus invites us to experience daily life as an endless chain of aha! moments – Brother Lawrence moments of ongoing worship and celebration; Mother Teresa moments of sacramental service in which we experience the mystery of his presence in the very people we encounter every day. He wants us to see him in the beggarly and bedraggled of the world, and he wants us to see him in the church – in each other's brokenness, presenting himself to us in another of his distressing disguises, in our own meanness and sin, that we might love him as he loves us.

The way of mystery is not nearly so strange and esoteric as some people make it out to be. It is, as Brother Lawrence so beautifully modeled, practicing the presence of Christ. We don't have to stress and strain ourselves to do this. We simply need to open our eyes and ears to what is presently all around us – *a new creation!*

15. Clay in the Potter's Hands

You turn things upside down, as if the potter were thought to be like the clay! Shall what is formed say to him who formed it, "He did not make me"? Can the pot say of the potter, "He knows nothing"?

Isaiah 29:16

Let faith be all eyes and ears. Surrender to God and let Him make His full impression on you, revealing Himself fully in your soul.
Andrew Murray, With Christ in the School of Prayer

Fleeting Fads and Fashions

I'm embarrassed whenever Dianne shows the old photograph to friends. It's a picture of me, standing alone in my parents' front yard wearing a purple cap and gown. It was the day of my high school graduation. Tufts of shoulder-length, auburn hair poured from the base of the cap, frizzing downward and outward. I was expressionless – as stone-faced as I was stoned. At the time I thought I looked cool. *I was cool.* All my friends thought so. In fact many of them sported similar hairstyles. It was after all the seventies – the days of miniskirts and muttonchops; bellbottoms and hot pants; caftans and afghans, platform sole shoes and trouser suits. What looked "normal" to us then looks costume-like now.

The feeling I have about that picture is not unique. Most people who saunter down memory lane by way of family photo albums know whereof I speak. We look at twenty- and thirty-year-old pictures of ourselves and wonder who these people were. Where was their sense of fashion? How could they have ever left the house with their hair looking

like that? And what about those neckties? They were thick
enough to be bibs. In my case they were bibs!

The fads and fashions or our age are so ubiquitous, so
all-consuming that no other way of dressing or driving or
dreaming ever occurs to us. Old fashions look odd to us
now, but the thought rarely strikes us that what's *in* today
will appear every bit as *out* tomorrow. The so-called "present
age," as Scripture describes it, is precisely that – it's so *present*
that its hold on us is virtually undetectable.

Elsewhere I likened culture to a container into which the
(time-transcending) truth of Christ is poured. I noted that
God's truth never occurs in an a-cultural vacuum. The same,
of course, is true of us. Culture – the present age replete with
all that is trendy and timely – functions like a mold, shaping
us into its image. The Apostle Paul says as much in Romans
12:2. He specifically uses the term that describes a mold
when speaking of this age. He wants us to be completely
clear that he is talking about the time and place we *now
occupy*, with all of its likes and dislikes, styles and stigmas.
He recognized that the most powerful forces in our lives
are the ones most invisible to us. Again Eugene Peterson's
paraphrase is instructive: "Don't become so well-adjusted
to your culture that you fit into it without even thinking."
When we fit into culture without even thinking about it, we
unconsciously allow it to *press us into its mold*.

Here Paul is presenting the only alternative scenario to
offering our bodies as living sacrifices and being transformed
by the renewing of our minds. Either we will be *conformed*
by the molding influences of the present age or we will be
transformed by renewed minds – by minds that have been
shaped and reshaped, like clay in the potter's hands, by
the moment-by-moment discipline of being conscious of the
mystery of Christ's presence. We do this, as we saw in the
last chapter, by consciously appropriating everything we
are and do – in the here-and-now moment of daily living
– to the glory of God. Jesus meets us in every moment we
sanctify to his glory. But he leaves the choice to be *conformed*
or *transformed* up to us.

In the final analysis, our lives are shaped far more by the hundreds of tiny moments that we daily sanctify to Christ's honor than by the great, heroic events that are few and far between. As I drive my car, I can either succumb to the influences of a rat-race culture, treating others on the road as they treat me, or I can appropriate my actions and attitudes as a driver to the glory of God. I'm driving down the freeway and notice that the person in the lane next to me wants to get over. I can either speed up and block her attempts to do so, or I can slow down and give her the room she needs to make a safe lane change – declaring in a breath prayer, "This, Lord Jesus, I do to your glory." Every such instant presents a new opportunity to yield ourselves to God's sculpting influence.

Occupying our Measure of Faith

The car-driving example implies that the discipline of discerning Christ's presence in our present circumstances is a solitary practice. It is that, to be sure – but not only that. Paul continues in Romans 12 by showing us how this practice feeds into our relationships with other followers of Christ. He says that we mustn't think of ourselves more highly than we ought to think. We do that by thinking we're better than other people or that we don't need others to get along in our spiritual journey. Instead, he says, we must think sensibly of ourselves "in accordance with the measure of faith God has given" us (Romans 12:3). He immediately explains what he means by "measure of faith," using our physical bodies as an example.

Just as each part of our bodies has a vital-but-different function, "so in Christ we who are many form one body, and each member belongs to all the others" (v. 5). To think of ourselves sensibly then is to reckon with two essential facts of our existence: our uniqueness as individual disciples and our interdependency with other Christ followers whose collective uniqueness is both complementary and essential to our own existence.

We are personally related to Jesus Christ and therefore make many individual choices as to how (or whether) we will encounter Christ in the daily moments of our lives. But we also occupy a specific "measure of faith" that no one else fills in the same way. We look to other of Paul's writings for help with the term "measure." In Ephesians 4:16, a passage that reflects several ideas parallel with Romans 12, Paul uses the word measure to describe the unique *place* that each of us occupies in the body of Christ. Think of a ruler, such as a yardstick, whose length is considered complete for what it is. The whole is made up of various measures; the individual measures together make the whole. If any measure is missing, the ruler is defective. We are complete disciples when we are connected to other disciples. Every measure is uniquely crafted by the risen Christ to fit with and complement the other measures.

Soaring in the Spirit

This brings us to a key vantage point in our quest to soar in the Spirit. We've been climbing a mountain together through these last chapters and have now come to a resting point at the summit. The panoramic view of the landscape below affords sufficient perspective to consider the reason for this book's title. Both the cover and title betray the obvious inspiration of Isaiah 40:28–31:

> Do you not know?
>   Have you not heard?
> The LORD is the everlasting God,
>   the Creator of the ends of the earth.
> He will not grow tired or weary,
>   and his understanding no one can fathom.
> He gives strength to the weary
>   and increases the power of the weak.
> Even youths grow tired and weary,
>   and young men stumble and fall;

but those who hope in the LORD
  will renew their strength.
They will soar on wings like eagles;
  they will run and not grow weary,
  they will walk and not be faint.

There's more behind the title than my desire to get many
people to buy and read the book.

The title, *Soaring in the Spirit*, was inspired by my mentor
and friend, Jim McClendon. He points out that there are four
identifiable stages in the Christian life. Each stage is marked
by one of the church's significant communal practices, which
occur at key points in our spiritual journey. The first stage is
introduction – our first encounter with the way of Christ. This,
says McClendon, is memorialized in the church's practice
of catechism. The second stage is *initiation* – the transition
point from our own way to the way of Christ. "Conversion"
is closely tied to this stage and baptism is the corresponding
practice. The third stage is *following*. McClendon equates this
with the biblical term discipleship and says that the church's
recurring practice of Eucharist marks this stage.

Many followers of Christ consider these three stages,
variously expressed in different traditions, to be all there is
to the Christian life. Yet there remains, says McClendon, a
less-recognized but vital fourth stage in our spiritual journey.
He describes it – in the spirit of Isaiah 40:31 – as *Christian
soaring*, and says that *corporate spiritual discernment* is the
corresponding practice.

McClendon admits that discernment of this sort has been
the exception more than the rule during the last 500 years
in which other forces set the church's agenda. And without
this practice of communal discernment, disciples have been
largely on their own in matters of discernment and spiritual
soaring. Mystics like Ignatius of Loyola, Teresa of Avila,
Brother Lawrence, John of the Cross, Madame Guyon, George
Fox, Thomas Merton, Mother Teresa, and Richard Foster are
outstanding figures precisely because each one exemplifies in
his or her own way a potent force of spirituality that has
been missed (and sometimes dismissed) by the mainstream.

The People of Discerning Communities

St. Paul in Romans 12 shows us what kind of individual is required if such communities of discernment are to exist and thrive. They are people who personally engage the mystery of Christ in their own daily lives. The practice of the presence of Christ in the moment-by-moment living of life is both *essential for* and *inspired by* discerning Christian community. When a community functions as a core model, it becomes the corporate embodiment of the ideals and convictions of the individuals who comprise the group. And *the collective expression* of the group's ideals and convictions is always greater than that of the individual members themselves.

Think of the "mob mentality" that incites a gathering of otherwise law-abiding citizens to overturn cars, smash storefront windows, and lock arms in protest until they are dragged off to jail by police dressed in riot gear. It's the snowball effect of their collective passions. The gathering of like-minded people creates a synergy that takes on a life of its own – a life that is bigger than the sum of its parts.

When Christians gather, the collective expression of the group is derived from the individual spirituality of its members. In every instance of core community the group feeds the individual and the individual feeds the group, which in turn feeds the individual, and so the cycle continues. We need not concern ourselves with the chicken-or-egg question. Scripture envisions the matter of individual and collective existence as a both–and affair. A follower of Christ needs the local church, and the local church needs the follower. But whether together or apart, we need to be about the business of engaging Christ's presence. Discerning individuals and discerning communities need and feed each other if they wish to soar in the Spirit.

We engage in the practice of corporate spiritual discernment in our collective worship, work, and witness. We gather for worship as people who have been individually practicing the presence of Christ in our daily lives. Jesus promises that when we gather, he too is with us. So what is the *collective expression* of this experience – the *worshipful synergy* that takes on a life of its own, a life greater than the sum of its parts? It is, in a word, *falling-down worship*. In his conversation with an unnamed Samaritan woman, Jesus spoke of New Testament worship. He said true worshipers worship God "in spirit and in truth." His Father *seeks out* those who worship in this way. "God is spirit," Jesus said, which means that he's not limited to a specific time and place. We need not go to Jerusalem on a certain feast day to worship God. Worshiping in spirit means that we enjoy a connection with God 24/7. Such worship is to be "in truth." There's no place for phoniness or façades. God sees right through us – he is after all spirit.[1]

What's particularly noteworthy about this passage is the word that the writer of the Fourth Gospel uses for "worship." It conveys the idea of falling down and prostrating ourselves before God. It's different than the word used in Romans 12. Paul in Romans 12 speaks of the intentioned consecration of our daily activities to the glory of God. In John 4 Jesus uses a term that describes *the human response to a divine encounter*. As Evelyn Underhill put it, worship "in all its grades and kinds, is the response of the creature to the Eternal."[2] When God shows up, we fall down.

People throughout the biblical narrative fell down when God showed up. Abraham fell down (Genesis 17:17). Balaam fell down (Numbers 22:31). Joshua fell down (Joshua 5:14). When the Spirit of the LORD spoke through Jahaziel son of Zechariah and assured King Jehoshaphat and all Judah that the victory would be theirs, Jehoshaphat and all Judah fell down in worship before the LORD (2 Chronicles 20:14–17). Ezekiel fell down on several occasions (Ezekiel 1:28; 3:23; 44:4). So did Daniel (Daniel 10:7–17). The twenty-four elders who sit in God's eternal presence fall down in worship at every hint of praise (Revelation 4:4–10).

Scripture teaches that when we come near to God, he comes near to us (James 4:8). This of course happens individually as well as corporately. When God broke into my consciousness as I sat on the deck those many years ago, I fell down (in every way but physically). When our cat, Smokey, returned home with a broken leg – a return miraculously timed in answer to Dianne's prayer – my family and I fell down. When we gather and experience the wonder of God's presence in community, however, the collective expression exceeds the sum of our individual falling-down experiences.

These experiences, if they are to be "in truth," cannot be contrived. Neither can we coerce them from God by "getting our worship right." There is a difference between the biblical meaning of *truth* and our human conception of *right*. But there are things that we bring to the table, which can either enhance or impede our corporate experiences of God's presence. One important prerequisite that we already considered is the practice of individual discernment, which is achieved by offering our bodies as living sacrifices and by which we perceive God's will in the *now* of daily living. This in turn enhances the possibility that we will gather with *a shared expectation* of encountering God together.

Our liturgies are best designed with both horizontal and vertical focuses. We begin with several one-another components that are designed to "re-member" us as the many-yet-one body of Christ. We "speak *to one another*," as Paul says, "in psalms and hymns and spiritual songs." We extend the peace of Christ to one another, we confess our sins to one another, and together we share the eucharistic meal of remembrance and hope. Then, with corporate solidarity duly reestablished, we lift our collective gaze heavenward, singing and making melody with true hearts to the Lord. As one, we draw near to God. And in that shared moment God draws close, and together we undergo a *new creation!* experience, a spiritual *aha!*, a collective *falling-down* that awakens us afresh to our place in the world as the people of God. With Isaiah we cry, "Here we are, send us!"

In discerning community we conceive of gathered work along the lines of our distinctive measures of faith. First, by Christ's faithful leading we discover our spiritual gifts together. Scripture promises that every disciple has at least one (1 Corinthians 12:7). Apostolic leadership in the local church is most true when it leads us into the discovery and implementation of these gifts (Ephesians 4:11, 12). Together we also discern the profound difference between consumer-style spirituality, which exalts the individual's felt needs, and

Christ-focused spirituality, which exalts the One who is going before us, leading us out to be his faithful witnesses.

As Jesus' disciples our collective discernment includes a component that is indispensable to our witness in the world – the capacity to recognize the many ways that the kingdom of God has already penetrated the domain of darkness.[3] Christ has already gone before us to make preparations for the feast. The witnessing activity associated with this facet of discernment is the "naming and claiming" of everything in our contemporary world that bears the marks of God's influence. The Apostle Paul named and claimed God's influence when he visited Athens.

Of course Paul was initially shocked by what he saw there. As he beheld that "city full of idols" for the first time, he was "greatly distressed." The original language says that his spirit was angered and grieved. That's understandable. He was raised a devout Jew. We learn elsewhere that he was tutored by Gamaliel, one of the most distinguished teachers of the Law (Acts 22:3). Before his dramatic conversion he was a member of the Pharisees, a sect known for its strict adherence to Jewish law and custom. As such, he persecuted followers of Christ "to their death, arresting both men and women and throwing them into prison" (Acts 22:4). In short, Paul did not take his convictions lightly. He was a man who was driven to act on what he believed. When God's reputation was on the line, he was not one to mince words.

Yet there he was in Athens. The ancient writer, Petronius, said that it was easier to find a god in Athens than a man. Some estimate that there were at least 30,000 gods in Athens at the time of Paul's visit. The sights and sounds of that place curled his fists and made the hair on the back of his neck stand up. The Jewish blood that coursed through his veins reached boiling point as he turned yet another corner and saw more idols. The opening words of the Ten Commandments chafed his conscience:

> I am the Lord your God, who brought you out of Egypt, out of the land of slavery. You shall have no other gods before me. You shall not make for yourself an image in the form of anything

in heaven above or on the earth beneath or in the waters below. You shall not bow down to them or worship them; for I, the LORD your God, am a jealous God (Exodus 20:2–4a)

It was more than his soul could bear. Like the prophet of old, in whose belly God's word burned like fire, Paul could not stay silent. But his approach to this strange set of circumstances is most instructive.

We might well imagine what Paul would have said to that crowd had he assumed the character of a Jeremiah or Amos. "Woe to you Athens, a city full of idols! You boast of great wisdom and knowledge, yet your worship of wood and stone betrays your foolishness. The Lord Most High, Creator of heaven and earth, declares that those who worship gods that cannot hear or see will become like them, neither hearing nor seeing. You are destined to ruin. Your wise men will long for a counselor but will find none. Your women and children will be led away in chains. Your fine buildings will be plundered and burned to the ground." But he did not say any of those things. He conducted himself as anything but a Jewish prophet.

Paul instead spoke to the Athenians as a philosopher. He "reasoned in the synagogue with both Jews and God-fearing Greeks, as well as in the marketplace day by day with those who happened to be there" (Acts 17:17). "Reason" in this text is the word from which we get "dialog." Paul did not preach at them. He engaged them in conversation. He had back-and-forth discussion with his audience. Paul would have likely offended some hard-line Christians today who believe that sin in every instance has to be confronted head on and crushed in its place. Paul did not water down the gospel by any means. He "preached the good news about Jesus and the resurrection" (v. 18). But he minded his manners. He showed respect and addressed these people as his equals. I suspect he smiled and even laughed with his conversation partners. Mind you, this group of Epicurean and Stoic philosophers was not particularly receptive to his message. Whatever Paul did, it worked. It got him into a meeting of the Areopagus, which was an invitation-only affair. And once there, Paul made the most of this opportunity.

Paul had spent several days quietly touring the city. He walked past the temple of the goddess Demeter, which featured statues of her and her daughter. And just down the way he saw the statues of Poseidon, Athena, Apollo, Hermes, and Zeus. He visited the altar of Mercy and the gymnasium of Ptolemy. Everywhere he turned there were more shrines; more idols. He was on sensory overload. But then he saw it. It was a *new creation!* moment; a spiritual *aha!* He silently thanked God for leading him to it – its inscription was displayed unremarkably. Passers-by might not even notice. Yet there it stood, as plain as day – a lone altar, bearing the insignia: *"To an Unknown God."* Paul stood there for several minutes, reading and rereading the inscription. It overwhelmed him. Amidst the very objects he repudiated most was a sign of God's presence. He now saw this city full of idols as God's place; under God's influence.

Standing at the Areopagus, Paul began his speech by smiling at his listeners and announcing that the host of idols in Athens clearly demonstrated one thing – *they were spiritually minded*. "It is plain to see," said Paul, "that you Athenians take your religion seriously. When I arrived here the other day, I was fascinated with all the shrines I came across" (Acts 17:23a). Paul was not being inauthentic. God enabled him to see something that his undiscerning eyes could never have seen before. The Athenians' many objects of worship pointed to the unmistakable evidence of God's influence in that benighted place. Rather than construing Athens' many gods negatively, Paul could now see them for what they were – humankind's attempts to be rightly related to the Divine. Then Paul segues, naming and claiming what is properly God's: "And then I found one inscribed, to the god nobody knows. I'm here to introduce you to this God so you can worship intelligently, and know who you're dealing with" (v. 23b).[4] He summarized the biblical creation story, quoted one of their poets, spoke of God's judgment on unbelief, and then described the resurrection of Jesus Christ.

Some of Paul's listeners were offended when he spoke of resurrection. That came as no surprise to Paul. He knew that the idea of human flesh being preserved in any form would be offensive to those who thought that the physical and spiritual worlds were incompatible. There is after all a point in every situation when certain aspects of Christ's truth will offend some. It's unavoidable. What Paul models in this situation, however, is that we don't lead with the most offensive parts of our witness. Instead, we take time to discern the points of convergence between a given culture and the truth of Christ. Then we name and claim what is already under God's influence so that our conversation partners can see that we value them and their world. They see that we're treating them as equals. We're not there to preach at them; we're there to dialog with them – and to receive as much from them as we hope they will gain from us. In this process of discernment and interchange, we too are changed and enriched.

God's influence is all around us if we pause to consider it. I'm standing in the checkout line at the local grocery store. The man a couple of people in front of me reaches into his pocket to get his money. A twenty-dollar bill falls to the floor. He doesn't notice. No one sees it except the single mother just behind him. The woman desperately needs the cash. She's been reduced to paying for her groceries with food stamps. This woman is not a churchgoing person. She has never professed faith in Christ. Yet there she stands, all alone in this moral dilemma. She doesn't hesitate. Keeping her back straight, she bends her knees and snatches the cash from the floor. Then just as quickly she rises and taps the stranger's shoulder, "Sir, you dropped this." Surprised, the man thanks her and takes back his money. The kingdom of God, Jesus says, is all around us. It is manifest in every act of kindness, every expression of good will, every act of mercy. It falls to discerning witnesses to see God's influence for what it is, and to invite others to recognize it as such and to embrace the One from whom every good and perfect gift comes.

Imprinting and Imperfections

This naming-and-claiming practice helps us to engage the present age while at the same time resisting its molding influence. But we must also reckon with the fact that this practice never makes us perfect. Would-be soarers are as blemished as nonsoarers. Soaring doesn't come to us instinctively and it is not something that is ever fully mastered this side of the resurrection. We can take our cue from the eagle, from which our image of spiritual soaring is derived. Surprisingly, flying does not come naturally to these majestic creatures – at least not at first. Like ducks and geese, eagles learn eagle-like behavior by watching their parents.

This phenomenon of learned behavior in certain animals is called "imprinting." The term was coined by Konrad Lorenz, one of the main founders of ethology, a branch of science that examines animal behavior, especially as it occurs in its native environment. The process of imprinting begins the moment a bird hatches from its egg. It latches onto the first moving object it sees, embracing it as its parent, and imitating its every move.

Lorenz recalled one occasion when a group of ducklings hatched while he was walking around them wearing a pair of boots. The chicks imprinted on the boots. From that point on, the ducks curled up at night on his vacant boots instead of retreating to their warm, safe nest. Whenever Lorenz put on the boots, they followed him (his boots, that is) wherever he went. For this reason, whenever rescued eagle eggs are hatched in a bird shelter, they are fed with an eagle-like glove to keep them from imprinting on the human feeder and resisting their own kind when they are eventually reintroduced to the wild.

Soaring is an acquired art for eagles and for followers of Jesus Christ. It is a matter of proper imprinting. Our present age imprints us to stay on the ground; the risen Christ re-imprints us to soar in the Spirit. Just as "birds of a feather flock together," so we who are transformed by the renewing of our minds soar together. But until Christ returns, we will continue to struggle with the fact of our dual imprinting. The best we can hope for, if we dare to be so honest, is that his re-imprinting work will free us to soar more often than not as we continue our journey.

The re-imprinting process is both individual and communal. Individually, Jesus reshapes us through the daily discipline of offering our bodies as living sacrifices. For the most part we engage in this discipline on our own, but it prepares us to be in community with each other in which the collective synergy is greater than the sum of our individual gifts and passions. St. Paul says that our gifts and passions are most effectively ignited when we are empowered to serve in ways that fit our unique "measure of faith." "If your gift is prophesying," Paul counsels, "then prophesy in accordance with your faith; if it is serving, then serve; if it is teaching, then teach; if it is to encourage, then give encouragement; if it is giving, then give generously; if it is to lead, do it diligently; if it is to show mercy, do it cheerfully" (Romans 12:6–8). The correspondence between the nature of our *gifts* and the nature of our *service* is unmistakable. When we are ministering in accordance with our designated measure, we will find ourselves soaring together in the Spirit. But such soaring does not come naturally. It requires the continued re-imprinting work of the risen Christ, which effectively changes the way we conceive of the church.

It is noteworthy that followers of Christ attain "the whole measure of the fullness of Christ" by means of what Ray C. Stedman calls "body life."[5] It should strike the modern mind as nothing less than scandalous, in fact, that spiritual soaring comes through the *practice* of communal engagement rather than the *study* of spiritual truth. Paul declares in Ephesians 4 that when we are engaged together in the ministries of our respective measures of faith, we "will no longer be infants, tossed back and forth by the waves, and blown here and there by every wind of teaching and by the cunning and craftiness of people in their deceitful scheming" (v. 14). The primary source of so-called doctrinal stability, in other words, is the communal engagement of our spiritual gifts, not sitting and listening to sermons.

The shape of each individual faith community is necessarily different from others, for no two constellations of disciples are exactly alike. It is also obvious that these gatherings are in a constant state of flux. While newcomers bring their own gifts to the mix, others as a matter of course move or pass away. This biblical pattern of church is very different than the cookie-cutter style we've grown so accustomed to in the West. And this is where the rub comes. Even so-called emergent churches have fallen into predictable patterns that cater to the individualistic sensibilities of religious consumers. We are compelled, it seems, to fashion church in the form of the market place, rather than as organic communities, whose mission and ministries in every case are shaped by the gifts and passions of the ones who make up each gathering. The molding, homogenizing work of the present age is alive and well.

Flawed but Faithful

We must remember, however, that our best attempts to follow the way of Christ are always flawed. Illusions of the church as a dynamic, organic community of discerning disciples – soaring wistfully in the Spirit as each one serves according to his or her measure of faith, worshiping and witnessing faithfully and effectively – crumble under the weight of the church's actual state. We weren't perfect in the first century and we won't be perfect when Christ returns at the end of the age. Nor do the mystics reflect lives of unencumbered spiritual soaring. Mother Teresa experienced her share of spiritual high points, but she also suffered repeated and prolonged dark nights of the soul. During one dark period she described the "terrible pain of loss, of God not wanting me, of God not being God, of God not really existing." Mother Teresa bent under the stress of these seasons, but by God's mercy and grace she did not break.

What keeps us from buckling under the false notions of "how things ought to be" is the ever-continuing fellowship of the One who promised never to leave or forsake us. Even when we are faithless, he will remain faithful, "for he cannot deny himself" (2 Timothy 2:13). The journey with Christ is neither painless nor perfect. We travel this road, after all, wearing cultural costumes; at times distracted, like Lorenz's ducks, by the boots of this present age. But to keep us from being crushed or hopelessly perplexed, God meets us in our flawed attempts to appropriate our waking moments to his glory and to mediate his grace to each other in community.

Undulating though it may be, our simple, wavering focus on Christ's smiling cross is sufficient. Slowly the risen Christ re-imprints us, making us malleable clay in the Potter's hands. Worldly fashions and false imprinting notwithstanding, the potter patiently, lovingly continues his labor long into the soul's dark night, shaping and reshaping us until at last his work is done. Then, in the light of new creation's last dawn, he rejoices and proudly holds us up, vessels of honor for all to see, exclaiming loudly enough for all heaven and earth to hear: "Well done, my good and faithful servants, you have been faithful with a few things. Now come and share your master's happiness."

Notes

1. Life After God

[1] "Mortal Sin," *Catechism of the Catholic Church* (Wichita, KS: Saint Jerome Press, 2004), #1874.
[2] "Venial Sin," *Catechism of the Catholic Church*, #1863.
[3] Perry D. LeFevre (ed.), *The Prayers of Kierkegaard* (Chicago: University of Chicago Press, 1956), p. 48.

2. Messy Spirituality

[1] "Novena" comes from the Latin word *novem*, which means "nine." It is a prayer that one says for nine consecutive days for the purpose of imploring God's favor or making a special petition.
[2] Mike Yaconelli, *Messy Spirituality* (Grand Rapids, MI: Zondervan, 2002), p. 10.
[3] C. S. Lewis, *The Screwtape Letters* (New York, NY: Macmillan, 1943), from Letter 8.
[4] Dietrich Bonhoeffer, *Cost of Discipleship* (New York, NY: Macmillan Publishing Company, 1963), p. 47.
[5] My friend, Brennan Manning, recently introduced me to another subtle but profoundly meaningful nuance of this passage. He noted that the word "remain" in this text conveys the idea of permanency. Elsewhere in the New Testament the word describes one's lodging or taking up (permanent) residence in a given place. With that in mind, Brennan said, "Jesus doesn't just want to pay us a visit. He wants to live with us . . . *forever*."
[6] Many scholars believe that Ephesians was actually an "encyclical epistle" that was written for distribution to several first-century congregations. Accordingly, Paul intended his thoughts here to go out to a wider audience than that of a single congregation.

[7] David F. Ford, *Self and Salvation: Being Transformed* (Cambridge: Cambridge University Press, 1999), observes that the message of Ephesians is "a testimony to the quality of transformed life in a worshiping community. Its horizon for human flourishing is unsurpassably vast . . . Within that, its special focus is on what it means to have a particular social identity in relation to God and other people" (pp. 107, 108).

3. Perils of Sin Management

[1] Brennan Manning, *The Ragamuffin Gospel* (Sisters, OR: Multnomah Publishers, 2000).

[2] Dallas Willard, *The Divine Conspiracy: Rediscovering Our Hidden Life in God* (New York, NY: HarperSanFrancisco, 1998), pp. 41, 42.

[3] The Roman Catholic confessional, Catholic and Protestant spiritual directors, and "accountability groups" (or "accountability partners") are just a few of several notable exceptions to the church's prevailing reluctance to confront and confess sin.

[4] The image of the lampstand comes from Revelation 2:5, in which the risen Christ warned the church of Ephesus to repent or face the consequences: "If you do not repent, I will come to you and remove your lampstand from its place." Scholars are divided as to what, specifically, the lampstand was intended to symbolize. In the light of 1:20, however, it would appear that the lampstand referred to the church itself. Accordingly, the removal of the lampstand would be nothing other than the removal of that particular congregation.

4. Spiders, Flames, and an Angry God

[1] Jonathan Edwards, "Sinners in the Hands of an Angry God" is available from, e.g., {http://edwards.yale.edu/images/pdf/sinners.pdf}.

[2] The Great Awakening was by no means monolithic. It consisted of a series of revivals that swept across the American colonies from Maine to Georgia during the eighteenth century. Signs of revival started to appear as early at 1679 in Northampton, Massachusetts under the preaching of Samuel Stoddard. A number of short-lived

revivals germinated but soon languished under the scorching winds of Enlightenment rationalism. Jonathan Edwards emerged as one of the most compelling voices in opposition to notions that human beings could think the thoughts of God without God's help. But Edwards' was not the only voice. Presbyterian preachers trained by William Tennet were largely responsible for the revivals that erupted in the Middle Colonies. Tennet's son, Gilbert, became a leading figure of these revivals. The famous Methodist preacher, George Whitefield, and the preachers who followed him, exerted much influence as well.

3 Jeff VanVonderen, *Tired of Trying to Measure Up* (Minneapolis, MN: Bethany House Publishers, 1989), p. 16.

4 VanVonderen, *Tired of Trying to Measure Up*, p. 17.

6. Belief on Steroids

1 Saint Anselm, *Monologion and Proslogion: With the Replies of Gaunilo and Anselm*, translated, with notes and introduction, by Thomas Williams (Indianapolis, Hackett Publishing Company, 1996), p. 99.

7. The "Most-Modern Age"

1 Stanley Eugene Fish, *Is There a Text in this Class? The Authority of Interpretive Communities* (Cambridge, MA: Harvard University Press, 1980).

2 Leonard Sweet, Andy Crouch, Brian McLaren, Erwin McManus, Michael Horton, and Frederica Mathewes-Green, *Church in the Emerging Culture: Five Perspectives* (Grand Rapids, MI: Zondervan Publishing House, 2003).

3 These criteria were popularized by Leonard Sweet in the acronym "EPIC." See Leonard Sweet, *Post-Modern Pilgrims: First Century Passion for the 21st Century World* (Nashville, TN: Broadman & Holman, 2000).

4 There are other reasons behind this reason. Those in the mid twentieth century who questioned the existence of basic beliefs were motivated to do so, at least in part, by a growing inhospitality toward the "inhumanity" of Newtonian science,

which effectively challenged the legitimacy of the whole modern program. This critique was first leveled 150 years earlier in England by poet and mystic, William Blake, and in Germany by playwright and poet, Friedrich Schiller.

[5] Stephen Toulmin, *Cosmopolis: The Hidden Agenda of Modernity* (Chicago, IL: The University of Chicago Press, 1990), pp. 22–44.

[6] Toulmin, *Cosmopolis*, pp. 22–44.

8. Beyond All Reasonable Doubt

[1] Moreover, scientists estimate that the total number of extinct bird species is far greater than that of non-extinct species.

[2] We refer to such people as "non-literate" instead of "illiterate" because the latter term implies that literacy is the cultural norm, which was not the case until it was necessitated by the widespread availability of reading material.

[3] David McDonald, "Prayground.TV," DMin Dissertation, George Fox University, 2006, p. 40. Cf. Pew Internet and American Life Project, *Wired Churches, Wired Temples: Taking Congregations and Missions into Cyberspace* [document online] (accessed December 20, 2005); available from {http://www.pewInternet.org/report_display.asp?r=28}.

[4] Without disrupting the flow of the discussion above, I wish to insert a word of caution regarding the use of statistical data. Numbers – nameless, faceless figures – comprise the foundation of quantitative analysis. When we appeal to statistical data as the sole means by which to assess a given dimension of human life, be it spiritual or otherwise, we run the risk of missing the story-formed subtleties and nuances that help us account for the complexities and potentially exceptional nature of the phenomena under our scrutiny. Quantitative analysts (and the rest of us who are enamored by numbers) face the ubiquitous temptation to read more into data than we can legitimately extrapolate from the data. Numbers, at the very most, tell only part of the story.

[5] Measures reflecting the sharpest declines between 1991 and 2001 were (1) Bible reading (falling from 45% to 37%), (2) church attendance (from 49% to 42%), (3) volunteering at church (from 27% to 20%), and (4) adult Sunday school attendance (from 23% to 19%). Barna Research Group Ltd, "Annual Study Reveals America is Spiritually Stagnant" (March 5, 2001), [document

online] (accessed May 1, 2007); available from http://www.barna. org/FlexPage.aspx?Page=BarnaUpdate&BarnaUpdateID=84.

6 Cf. Richard Tarnas, *The Passion of the Western Mind: Understanding the Ideas That Have Shaped Our World View* (New York: Ballantine Books, 1991), pp. 175–178. John B. Cobb, Jr. observes that Western higher education is clearly the product of the church: "The universities were creatures of the church. Theology was the queen of the sciences. They educated not only clergy but other professionals as well. Also the education was what we would call today broadly humanistic. But all of this was understood as in the service of Christendom." Cobb observes that well into the modern period, "university education in Europe remained much what it had been in the high Middle Ages." In fact, the vestiges of the original and primary goals of university education were apparent as late as the mid-twentieth century. Drawing from his teaching experience at the University of Mainz in the 1960s, Cobb muses: "I was struck also by the fact that the humanistic gymnasia through which students prepared for entry into the university taught them Greek and Latin and even Hebrew, *just those languages most needed for a classical theological education*" (my emphasis). In John B. Cobb, Jr., "Higher Education and the Periodization of History," *Religion On-Line* [document online] (accessed November 8, 2006); available from {http://www. religion-online.org/showarticle.asp?title=372}.

7 Such benefits include solid works in systematic theology and Christian apologetics, as exemplified in the works of both Roman Catholic and Protestant scholars. See, for example, John Henry Newman, *Apologia Pro Vita Sua* (New York: The Modern Library, 1950), *An Essay on the Development of Christian Doctrine* (London: James Toovey, 1845); Hans Küng, *Theology for the Third Millennium: An Ecumenical View*, trans. Peter Heinegg (New York and London: Doubleday, 1988), Avery Dulles, *The Craft of Theology: From Symbol to System* (New York: The Crossroad Publishing Company, 1992); Karl Barth's multi-volume magnum opus, *Church Dogmatics* – cf. Karl Barth, *Dogmatics in Outline*, trans. G. T. Thomson (London: SCM Press, 1949); Charles Hodge, *Systematic Theology* (Grand Rapids, MI: William B. Eerdmans Publishing Company, 1981); Carl F. H. Henry, *God, Revelation and Authority*, 6 vols (Waco, TX: Word Publishing, 1976 – 1983); Josh McDowell, *Evidence that Demands a Verdict: Historical Evidences for the Christian Faith* (San Bernardino, CA: Here's Life Publishers Inc., 1972). The list is long.

[8] For Anselm the whole of the intellectual enterprise is encapsulated in the phrase, "faith seeking understanding" (*fides quaerens intellectum*). He believed that truth could be had in no other way.

[9] Two classic contributions to this genre are William R. Bright, *Ten Basic Steps Toward Christian Maturity* (Arrowhead Springs, San Bernardino, CA: Campus Crusade for Christ International, 1964) and *Teacher's Manual for the Ten Basic Steps Toward Christian Maturity* (Arrowhead Springs, San Bernardino, CA: Campus Crusade for Christ International, 1965), in which the author claims that nearly "every major doctrine of the Christian faith has been carefully considered and clearly presented so that any person sincerely seeking spiritual truth will be generously rewarded by even a casual reading of these pages" (from *Teacher's Manual*, p. i). These works established a methodological paradigm for discipleship that influenced several generations of "disciple makers." The discipling practices that emerged from this paradigm consisted largely of guiding persons through select books or manuals, at the end of which exercise one was considered to have been duly "discipled." Cf. Francis M. Cosgrove, Jr., *Essentials of Discipleship* (Colorado Springs, CO: Navpress, 1980) and *A Bible Study on Essentials of Discipleship* (Colorado Springs, CO: Navpress, 1980).

[10] Jim Petersen, *Lifestyle Discipleship* (Colorado Springs, CO: Navpress, 1993), p. 15.

[11] And such black-and-white thinking dies hard, as evidenced by the fact that it was not until 1992 that the Vatican finally pardoned Galileo and officially admitted that he had been right all along.

9. A New Creation!

[1] Brother Lawrence, *The Practice of the Presence of God*, edited by Harold J. Chadwick (Gainesville, FL: Bridge-Logos Publishers, 1999), p. 14.

[2] Brother Lawrence, *The Practice of the Presence of God*, p. 15.

[3] Mother Teresa, *Total Surrender*, edited by Angelo Devananda (Ann Arbor, MI: Servant Publications, 1985), pp. 116, 117, 130, 139, 150.

[4] Berkeley A. Mickelsen, *Interpreting the Bible* (Grand Rapids, MI: Wm. B. Eerdmans Publishing Company, 1963).

5 A causal meaning of the Greek preposition *eis* is nowhere attested in Koine Greek.

6 The Greek preposition *epi* ("on" or "upon") is used, rather than the more common preposition used in the phrase, "in the name of" – *en*: "*Petros de pros autous metanoēsate, [phēsin,] kai baptisthētō hekastos humōn epi tō onomati Iēsou Christou eis aphesin tōn hamartiōn humōn*"

7 ωπἰ τὄ ονοματἰ τἰνοο,

8 William F. Arndt and F. Wilbur Gingrich, *A Greek-English Lexicon of the New Testament and Other Early Christian Literature*, 2nd edition (Chicago, IL: University of Chicago Press, 1979), p. 288.

9 Cf. George Raymond Beasley-Murray, *Baptism in the New Testament* (Grand Rapids, MI: Wm. B. Eerdmans Publishing Company, 1973).

10. Overthrow of the Mystics

1 Carole Spencer, PhD, email exchange, December 28, 2006.

2 Louis Cognet, *Le Crépuscule des Mystiques* (Tournai, Belgium: Desclée, 1958), introduction. See also Louis Bouyer, *The Christian Mystery: From Pagan Myth to Christian Mysticism*, translated by Illtyd Trethowan (Edinburgh: T. & T. Clark, 1990), pp. 260, 261; Bouyer, *A History of Christian Spirituality*, Vol. III (New York: The Seabury Press, 1969), p. 57.

3 Kevin Corrigan and Michael Harrington, "Pseudo-Dionysius the Areopagite," in *Stanford Encyclopedia of Philosophy* [document online] (accessed December 30, 2006); available from {http://plato.stanford.edu/entries/pseudo-dionysius-areopagite/}. Corrigan and Harrington go on to observe, "Dionysius represents his own teaching as coming from a certain Hierotheus and as being addressed to a certain Timotheus. He seems to conceive of himself, therefore, as an in-between figure, very like a Dionysius the Areopagite, in fact. Finally, if Iamblichus and Proclus can point to a primordial, pre-Platonic wisdom, namely, that of Pythagoras, and if Plotinus himself can claim not to be an originator of a tradition (after all, the term Neoplatonism is just a convenient modern tag), then why cannot Dionysius point to a distinctly Christian theological and philosophical resonance in an earlier pre-Plotinian wisdom that instantaneously bridged the gap between Judaeo-Christianity (St. Paul) and Athenian paganism (the Areopagite)?" It also bears mentioning that the synchronic

self-identification with biblical characters is attested in Scripture itself. The author of Ecclesiastes clearly identifies him-/herself with King Solomon. Yet internal evidence – namely, the book's style and vocabulary – suggests that it was written centuries after Solomon's death, sometime during the post-exilic period.

4   The mystic, Julian of Norwich (1342–1416), also quotes from his works three times.

5   Dionysius, *Mystical Theology*, chapter one, "What is the Divine Darkness?" in Colm Luibheid (ed.), *Pseudo-Dionysius: The Complete Works* (New York: Paulist Press, 1987), p. 137.

6   Jeffrey Stout, *The Flight from Authority: Religion, Morality, and the Quest for Autonomy* (Notre Dame, IN: University of Notre Dame Press, 1981), p. 41.

7   Bouyer, *A History of Christian Spirituality*, Vol. III, p. 57. Quakerism, of which George Fox is the celebrated founder, is the foremost of Protestant mystical movements.

8   John Howard Yoder, *The Priestly Kingdom: Social Ethics as Gospel* (Notre Dame, IN: The University of Notre Dame Press, 1984), p. 69.

11. Christianity à la Carte

1   Dallas Willard, *The Divine Conspiracy: Rediscovering Our Hidden Life in God* (New York: HarperSanFrancisco, 1998), p. 308 (my emphasis).

2   Michael C. Armour and Don Browning, *Systems-Sensitive Leadership: Empowering Diversity without Polarizing the Church* (Joplin, MO: College Press Publishing Company, 1995), pp. 16, 17.

3   Roland H. Bainton, "The Enduring Witness: The Mennonites," *Mennonite Life*, vol. 9, no. 2 (April 1954), pp. 83–90 (p. 89).

4   Robert Bellah and his colleagues credit seventeenth-century philosopher John Locke as the progenitor of this conception of human existence: "John Locke is the key figure and one enormously influential in America. The essence of the Lockean position is an almost ontological individualism. The individual is prior to society, which comes into existence only through the voluntary contract of individuals trying to maximize their own self-interest" (my emphasis). Robert N. Bellah, Richard Madsen, William M. Sullivan, Ann Swidler, and Steven M. Tipton, *Habits of the Heart: Individualism and Commitment in American Life* (New York: Harper & Row Publishers, 1985), p. 143.

5 John Locke, "A Letter Concerning Toleration," in *The Works of John Locke, A New Edition, Corrected*, Vol. VI (Aalen, Germany: Scientia Verlag, 1963), p. 13.

6 According to Roger Swagler, "consumerism" is a recent term that was coined in obscurity and has a variety of meanings. The consumer movement, for example, adopted the term to describe its activities. However, the general public has tended to respond very negatively to it, construing consumerism as the unduly pursuit of self-fulfillment by means of an excessive acquisition of material goods. Cf. Roger Swagler, "Evolution and Applications of the Term Consumerism: Theme and Variations," *Journal of Consumer Affairs*, 28, 2 (December 1994): 347. Similar excesses are attested in antiquity – in ancient Egypt, Babylon, Greece, and Rome, for example. But in the modern era, consumerism became much more commonplace among the masses. As the affluence of Western capitalism reached non-Western population centers like Tokyo, Hong Kong, Shanghai, Seoul, Taipei, Delhi, and Johannesburg, consumerism grew into a global phenomenon. For our purposes here, Steve Forward appropriately captures the spiritual overtones of this ideology: "Consumerism is a religious system that focuses on the accumulation of things and experiences; promising the answers to life's questions of meaning, purpose, identity and belonging through this process of consumption." (Steve Forward, "Consumerism – a Spiritual Quest," *Incite*, 43, p. 2 [document online] (accessed December 3, 2006); available from {http://www.tear.org.au/resources/incite/43/pdf/43.pdf})

7 To be sure, a general distortion of pastoral identity had been underway from the second century on when the church ascribed ontological significance to ordination in which the *persona* of the priest was seen as an icon of Christ. Anthony E. Harvey calls such a view disturbing, "in that the thrust of Jesus' teaching suggests that no such mediation is necessary; moreover, there is no trace of any priestly institution in the early years of the church that he founded." (A. E. Harvey, "Priesthood," in *The Oxford Companion to Christian Thought*, edited by Adrian Hastings [New York: Oxford University Press, 2000, p. 565]. The absence of biblical precedent for the priesthood notwithstanding, Harvey maintains that it has value as "a metaphor for a profound religious experience." One could therefore say that the modern church's understanding of pastoral ministry represents a modern departure from the apostolic norm reflected in Scripture.

8   Thomas C. Oden, *Pastoral Theology: Essentials of Ministry* (New York: HarperCollins Publishers, 1972 [1961]), p. 4. According to Oden, "The most astonishing example of this confusion of pastoral identity is the modern pastoral counseling, in which extensive professionalization has been attempted under the confusing rubric of pastor. The shingle of the therapist has been borrowed and put up, often with radical loss of anything resembling historical pastoral identity. The resulting irony is an attempt at a new profession that names itself by a name ('pastoral' counselor) whose meaning has been curiously forgotten."

9   Wes Roberts and Glenn Marshall, *Reclaiming God's Original Intent for the Church* (Colorado Springs, CO: NavPress, 2004), p. 145.

10 According to Leonard Sweet at last count there were more than 10,000 books in print that have "leadership" in the title. Accordingly, he asks, "Is it possible to bear one more without an authorial apology or excuse? Besides, what are the differences between a book on leadership by a Christian and one by Jack Welch? How many more books can you read based on the same formula: Follow these principles and you will change your life? The best reaction to the appearance of another leadership principle is one of resignation – another point nicely made but another instance of missing the point." Leonard Sweet, *Summoned to Lead* (Grand Rapids, MI: Zondervan, 2004), p. 16.

11 Ben Patterson, "The Call to Ministry, in *Leadership Handbook of Management and Administration*, edited by James D. Berkeley (Grand Rapids, MI: Baker Books, 1994), pp. 19, 20.

12 Revivalism's influence was far reaching, extending even into faith traditions that had maintained their distinctive identity as communities of discernment throughout most of the nineteenth century. The most notable example is the Quakers, which by the early twentieth century had divided into two distinct camps – the "orthodox" group that adhered to the "unprogrammed" format, in which disciples wait in silence for the direction of the risen and present Christ, and the "evangelical" or "pastoral" camp that ultimately adopted the forms of worship characteristic of most other evangelical churches.

13 Cf. Walter Rauschenbusch, *Christianity and the Social Crisis* (New York: Macmillan, 1907), and *A Theology for the Social Gospel* (New York: Macmillan, 1917).

14 For an excellent treatment of the pervasive influences of democracy on American Christianity, see Nathan O. Hatch, *The Democratization of American Christianity* (New Haven, CT:

Yale University Press, 1989). To be sure, the influences of this Arminian shift inspired by Methodist pietism were by no means uniform. As George Marsden observes, the union of revivalism and Arminian-directed pietism spawned in the unrestrained American context "innumerable variations of Calvinist and Arminian theology multiplied by countless varieties of denominational and revivalist emphases. The Calvinists tended to stress intellectual the importance of right doctrine, the cognitive aspects of faith, and higher education. On the other hand, more pietistically and emotionally oriented groups, such as the Methodists, tended to shun intellectual rigor and to stress the practical and experiential aspects of faith. Yet many groups in America stressed both the intellectual and the experiential-practical aspects." (George M. Marsden, *Fundamentalism and American Culture: The Shaping of Twentieth Century Evangelicalism, 1870–1925* (New York: Oxford University Press, 1980), p. 44)

15 As opposed to "limited atonement," which was embedded in the theology associated with the Great Awakening and underscored the belief that the benefits and blessings of Christ's sacrifice extend only to those whom God has foreordained.

16 Alistair Mason, "Arminianism," in *The Oxford Companion to Christian Thought*, edited by Adrian Hastings, Alistair Mason, and Hugh Pyper (New York: Oxford University Press, 2000), p. 41.

12. Church's Dual Citizenship

1 Historian Monroe Hawley identifies several such "heretical groups" who were probably closer to the truth than the dominant church – groups that were misrepresented by the standard account, which was conceived by those in positions of churchly power. Such groups, according to Hawley, include the Paulicians, Bogomils, Waldenses, Unitas Fratrum, and the Anabaptists. Cf. Monroe Hawley, *The Focus of our Faith: A New Look at the Restoration Principle* (Nashville, TN: 20th-Century Christian Foundation, 1985), pp. 29–38.

13. What Now?

[1] Ray S. Anderson, *The Shape of Practical Theology: Empowering Ministry with Theological Praxis* (Downers Grove, IL: InterVarsity Press, 2001), pp. 104–7.

[2] Gerald R. McDermott, "What if Paul Had Been from China? Reflections on the Possibility of Revelation in Non-Christian Religions," in *No Other Gods before Me? Evangelicals and the Challenge of World Religions*, edited by John G. Stackhouse, Jr. (Grand Rapids, MI: Baker Academic, 2001), pp. 17–35. McDermott says, "When we fail to recognize the development of doctrine both within Scripture and by the Spirit's gradual illumination of Scripture in church history, we begin to think we are in control of the gospel. We fail to see that Scripture is vast and rich, unsystematic and various, often figurative and indirect, so that 'to the end of our days and the church, it will be unexplored and unsubdued land.' When we fail to recognize the development of doctrine, we think we need only apply our previous understandings to the new situation rather than continually listening to God through fresh readings of God, Scripture, and world. Such listening is open to new understandings of the gospel, not just application of old understandings" (p. 21, my emphasis).

[3] Andrew F. Walls, *The Missionary Movement in Christian History* (Maryknoll, NY: Orbis, 1996), p. 173.

[4] McDermott, "What if Paul Had Been from China?," pp. 18–23.

[5] Thomas C. Oden, *After Modernity . . . What?* (Grand Rapids, MI: Zondervan Publishing House, 1990), p. 55.

[6] Edwin E. Aubrey, *Secularism a Myth: An Examination of the Current Attack on Secularism* (New York: Harper & Brothers, 1954), p. 30.

[7] Julian N. Hartt, *A Christian Critique of American Culture* (New York: Harper & Row, 1967), pp. 300, 301.

[8] James Wm. McClendon, *Witness: Systematic Theology, Volume 3* (Nashville, TN: Abingdon Press, 2000), pp. 418–20.

[9] In the mid-1990s Stan Grenz described the "postmodern phenomenon" in singular terms. He said that it "refers to the intellectual mood and cultural expressions that are becoming increasingly dominant in contemporary society . . . [and] we must pinpoint in greater detail what the postmodern phenomenon entails." He went on to say that the postmodern "ethos" is best accounted for as a loss of centeredness that shows up in "postmodern architecture," "postmodern art," "postmodern theater," and "postmodern fiction." However, we have now gained

more distance on this "phenomenon," and have come to recognize that centerlessness serves as a partial description at most.

[10] To be sure, there are many aspects of the so-called postmodern age that are actually *most* modern – such as the belief that all things modern are bad and that the best way forward is to extricate ourselves from modernity once and for all. To make such a plea for novelty is in fact the quintessence of the modern spirit.

[11] I feel compelled to point out with a smile – that the propensity to name our age is a very "modern" thing to do. Imagine people getting out of bed in the early sixteenth century and exclaiming, "Hey, we just entered the Renaissance . . . cool!"

[12] Chuck Colson, for example, claims that "postmodernism" is "the philosophy that claims there is no transcendent truth." Chuck Colson, "The Postmodern Crackup: from Soccer Moms to College Campuses, Signs of the End," *Christianity Today*, 47, 12 (December 2003), p. 72.

[13] This schism has never been more apparent among members of the Evangelical Theological Society, which approved at its 2004 annual meeting the following statement: "For the purpose of advising members regarding the intent and meaning of the reference to biblical inerrancy in the ETS Doctrinal Basis, the Society refers members to the Chicago Statement on Biblical Inerrancy (1978). The case for biblical inerrancy rests on the absolute trustworthiness of God and Scripture's testimony to itself. A proper understanding of inerrancy takes into account the language, genres, and intent of Scripture. We reject approaches to Scripture that deny that biblical truth claims are grounded in reality." ETS did this to remedy what it sensed as a slide to the (postmodern) left by some of its members. However, former ETS president Norman Geisler, a staunch proponent of biblical inerrancy and outspoken opponent of ETS members who take a softer view on the matter, said that the approving of such a statement is "little more than a Band-Aid on cancer." Norman L. Geisler, "A Band-Aid on Cancer: Comments on the Recent ETS Decision to Accept ICBI Statement" (November 29, 2004) [document online] (accessed May 3, 2005); available from {http://www.ses.edu/NormGeisler/ets2004.htm}.

[14] For an excellent treatment of this trend in emerging worship, cf. Robert Webber, *Ancient-Future Faith: Rethinking Evangelicalism for a Postmodern World* (Grand Rapids, MI: Baker Books, 1999), pp. 97–120.

[15] As reported in Robert C. Fuller, *Spiritual, But Not Religious: Understanding Unchurched America* (New York: Oxford University Press, 2001). Ironically, even though some are inclined to associate this phenomenon with so-called postmodernism, Fuller correctly argues that it is more likely due to the abiding influence of modern dualism: "Before the 20th century the terms religious and spiritual were used more or less interchangeably. But a number of modern intellectual and cultural forces have accentuated differences between the 'private' and 'public' spheres of life. The increasing prestige of the sciences, the insights of modern biblical scholarship, and greater awareness of cultural relativism all made it more difficult for educated Americans to sustain unqualified loyalty to religious institutions. Many began to associate genuine faith with the 'private' realm of personal experience rather than with the 'public' realm of institutions, creeds, and rituals. The word spiritual gradually came to be associated with a private realm of thought and experience while the word religious came to be connected with the public realm of membership in religious institutions, participation in formal rituals, and adherence to official denominational doctrines." (p. 5)

[16] Brian Zinnbauer, Kenneth Pargament, et al., "Religion and Spirituality: Unfuzzying the Fuzzy," *Journal for the Scientific Study of Religion* 36 (December, 1997), pp. 549–64 (p. 561, my emphasis).

[17] Fuller, *Spiritual, But Not Religious*, p. 7.

[18] Experts have identified "holism" as a recurring theme in the emerging age. Cf. Nancey Murphy and James Wm. McClendon, Jr. "Distinguishing Modern and Postmodern Theologies," *Modern Theology* 5, 3 (April 1989), pp. 191–214. However, holism in this sense is not to be equated with synthesis, which is what Fuller implies. Many people these days are quite content to embrace an assortment of beliefs that are inharmonious, having no apparent logical coherence.

14. The Way of Mystery

[1] Tucker N. Callaway, *Zen Way, Jesus Way* (Rutland, VT: C. E. Tuttle, 1987).

[2] Brennan Manning, *Ruthless Trust: The Ragamuffin's Path to God* (San Francisco, CA: HarperSanFrancisco, 2000, p. 50).

3 Here is a small, representative sample of such works. Suzanne G. Farnham, *Listening Hearts: Discerning Call in Community* (Harrisburg, PA: Morehouse Publishers, 1991); Ben Campbell Johnson, *Discerning God's Will* (Grand Rapids, MI: W. B. Eerdmans, 1990); Henry T. Blackaby, *Experiencing God: How to Live the Full Adventure of Knowing and Doing the Will of God* (Nashville, TN: Broadman & Holman Publishers, 1998); Sinclair B. Ferguson, *Discovering God's Will* (Carlisle, PA. The Banner of Truth Trust, 1994), Michael R. Tucker, *Live Confidently. How to Know God's Will* (Wheaton, IL: Tyndale House Publishers, 1976); Gordon T. Smith, *Listening to God in Times of Choice: The Art of Discerning God's Will* (Downers Grove, IL: InterVarsity Press, 1997); Haddon W. Robinson, *Decision-Making by the Book: How to Choose Wisely in an Age of Options* (Grand Rapids, MI: Discovery House, 1998); Garry Friesen, *Decision Making and the Will of God: A Biblical Alternative to the Traditional View* (Portland, OR: Multnomah Press, 1980).

4 Cf. Monteze Snyder, *Building Consensus: Conflict and Unity* (Richmond, IN: Earlham Quaker Foundations of Leadership Program, 2001); Anthony Bradney, *Living without Law: an Ethnography of Quaker Decision-Making, Dispute Avoidance, and Dispute Resolution* (Aldershot, England; Burlington VT: Ashgate, 2000); Michael J. Sheeran, *Beyond Majority Rule: Voteless Decisions in the Religious Society of Friends* (Philadelphia: Philadelphia Yearly Meeting of the Religious Society of Friends, 1983).

5 The term *logikos* means "rational," "reasonable," "thoughtful." The term *latreia* means "worship" or "service" generally, and in certain instances "priestly service." Cf. also Hebrews 9:6.

15. Clay in the Potter's Hands

1 "Etymologically ἀλήθεια [*alētheia*] has the meaning of non-concealment. It thus indicates a matter or state to the extent that it is seen, indicated or expressed, and that in such seeing, indication or expression it is disclosed, or discloses itself, as it really is, with the implication, of course, that it might be concealed, falsified, truncated, or suppressed. ἀλήθεια, therefore, denotes the 'full or real state of affairs.'" Gerhard Kittel, *Theological Dictionary of the New Testament*, Volume I, translated and edited by Geoffrey W. Bromiley (Grand Rapids, MI: Wm. B. Eerdmans Publishing Company, 1964), p. 238.

[2] Evelyn Underhill, *Worship* (New York: Harper & Brothers Publishers, 1936), p. 3.

[3] One of the great theological mistakes of late twentieth-century Protestant church was equating "the church" with "the kingdom of God." The most influential advocate of this position was George Eldon Ladd. He said, for example, that "the Kingdom of God which in the Old Testament dispensation was manifested in Israel is now working in the world through the Church." George Eldon Ladd, *The Gospel of the Kingdom: Scriptural Studies in the Kingdom of God* (London: Paternoster Press, 1959), p. 117.

[4] *The Message.*

[5] Cf. Ray C. Stedman, *Body Life* (Glendale, CA: Regal, 1972).

Series Titles Currently Available

Atonement for a 'Sinless' Society
Engaging with an emerging culture

Atonement for a 'Sinless' Society

Engaging with an Emerging Culture

Alan Mann

'Sin doesn't really exist as a serious idea in modern life,' wrote the journalist Bryan Appleyard. He is not alone in his views. 'Sin' has become just as tainted, polluted and defiled in the postmodern mind as the word itself indicates.

Atonement for a 'Sinless' Society is about an encounter between two stories: the story of the postmodern, post-industrialized, post-Christian 'sinless' self and the story of atonement played out in the Passion Narrative. Alan Mann charts a way through the apparent impasse between a story that supposedly relies on sin and guilt to become meaningful, and one that fails to recognize the plight of humanity as portrayed in this way. He shows how the biblical narrative needs to be reread in the light of this emerging story so that it can speak meaningfully and sufficiently to an increasingly 'sinless' society.

'Clear, creative, deep, compelling and inspiring' – **Brian D. McLaren**, author, speaker, networker

'Alan Mann's voice is needed and welcome . . . A penetrating analysis of the world we inhabit.' – **Joel B. Green**, Asbury Theological Seminary

'An insightful, timely and creative view of the atonement for our postmodern times.' – **Steve Chalk**, Oasis Trust

978-1-84227-355-5

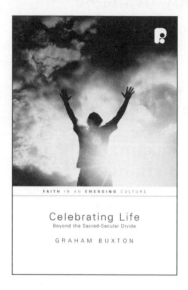

Celebrating Life

Beyond the Sacred-Secular Divide

Graham Buxton

As Christians, our engagement with the world and with culture is often impoverished as a result of unbiblical dualisms. More than we realise, the divide between sacred and secular is reinforced in our minds, contributing to an unhealthy and, at times, narrow super-spirituality. Seeking a more postmodern, holistic and, ultimately, more *Christian* approach to culture, Graham Buxton leads us on a journey towards the celebration of life in *all* its dimensions.

The first part of the book examines the roots of our dualistic thinking and its implications for culture. Part Two draws us from dualism to holism in a number of chapters that consider our engagement with literature, the creative arts, science, politics and business. Part Three draws the threads together by setting out the dimensions of a more holistic theology of the church's engagement with, and participation in, contemporary society that will lead us 'beyond the sacred-secular divide'.

'This is incarnational theology at its best!' – **Ray S. Anderson**, Senior Professor of Theology and Ministry, Fuller Theological Seminary, California.

Graham Buxton is Director of Postgraduate Studies in Ministry and Theology, Tabor College, Adelaide, Australia. He is author of Dancing in the Dark and The Trinity, Creation and Pastoral Ministry.

978-1-84227-507-1

Forthcoming Series Titles

Re:Mission

Biblical Mission for a Post-Biblical Church

Andrew Perriman

In this innovative and radical book postmodern mission and New Testament studies collide. Andrew Perriman examines the mission of the earliest church in its historical context and argues that our context is very different and *so our mission cannot simply be a matter of doing exactly what the earliest church did*. The key question at the heart of the book is, 'How do we shape a *biblical* theology of mission for a *post-biblical* church?'

> '*Re:Mission* distinguishes Perriman as a scholar who must be reckoned with in this time of rethinking and transition. A great piece of work!" – **Brian D. McLaren**, author (brianmclaren.net)

> 'Andrew Perriman has addressed one of the most challenging facets of New Testament teaching and he does so with remarkable insight and creativity. This fascinating book makes for urgent reading. – **Craig A. Evans**, Payzant Distinguished Professor of New Testament, Acadia Divinity College, Canada

Andrew Perriman lives in Holland and works with Christian Associates seeking to develop open, creative communities of faith for the emerging culture in Europe. He is author of *Speaking of Women* about Paul's teaching on women, *Faith, Health and Prosperity*, and, *The Coming of the Son of Man: New Testament Eschatology for an Emerging Church*.

978-1-84227-545-0

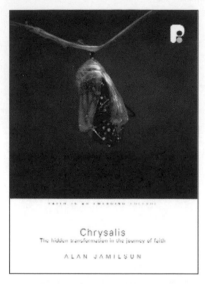

Chrysalis

The Hidden Transformation in the Journey of Faith

Alan Jamieson

Increasing numbers of Christian people find their faith metamorphosing. Substantial and essential change seems to beckon them beyond the standard images and forms of Christian faith but questions about where this may lead remain. Is this the death of personal faith or the emergence of something new? Could it be a journey that is Spirit-led?

Chrysalis uses the life-cycle of butterflies as a metaphor for the faith journey that many contemporary people are experiencing. Drawing on the three main phases of a butterfly's life and the transformations between these, the book suggests subtle similarities with the zones of Christian faith that many encounter. For butterflies and Christians change between these '*phases*' or '*zones*' is substantial, life-changing and irreversible.

This book accompanies ordinary people in the midst of substantive faith change. It is an excellent resource for those who choose to support others through faith transformations. *Chrysalis* is primarily pastoral and practical drawing on the author's experience of accompanying people in the midst of difficult personal faith changes.

Alan Jamieson is a minister in New Zealand and a trained sociologist. His internationally acclaimed first book, *A Churchless Faith*, researched why people leave their churches to continue their walk of faith outside the church.

978-1-84227-544-3

Metavista

Bible, Church and Mission in an Age of Imagination

Colin Green and Martin Robinson

The core narrative of the Christian faith, the book that conveys it (the Bible) and the institution of the church have all been marginalised by the development of modernity and post-modernity. Strangely, post-modernity has created an opportunity for religious thinking and experience to re-enter the lives of many. Yet, despite its astonishing assault on modernity, post-modernity is not itself an adequate framework for thinking about life. There is therefore a new opportunity for Christians to imagine what comes *after* post-modernity and to prepare the church, its book and its story for a new engagement of mission with western culture. The church on the margins, through a creative missionary imagination can audaciously re-define the centre of western cultural life. This book will attempt to sketch what such an approach might look like

'If you have a taste for the subversive, a passion for the church, a heart for biblical engagement, and an eye on the future; this book is a must-read.'
– **Roy Searle**, Northumbria Community, former President of the Baptist Union of Great Britain

Colin Greene is Professor of Theological and Cultural Studies at Mars Hill Graduate School in Seattle. He is author of *Christology in Cultural Perspective*.
Martin Robinson is an international speaker, a writer, and Director of 'Together in Mission'.

978-1-84227-506-1